Laughing in a Waterfall

Laughing
in a
Waterfall

A MOTHER'S MEMOIR

Susie,
Keep laughing!
Marianne Dietzel

Marianne Dietzel

Laughing Bridge Publishing
St. Paul, Minnesota

Published by:
Laughing Bridge Publishing
www.mariannedietzel.com

To all named and unnamed family and friends who are a part of this story, I ask forgiveness if parts of the story are remembered differently or not included.

Poems, letters and photographs are used with permission.

Cover painting, "For Nina at One Year," by Laura Summer
Book design: Dorie McClelland, Spring Book Design
First edition.
Printed in the United States of America.
15 14 13 12 1 2 3 4

ISBN: 978-0-615-37175-7

In loving memory of
Nina Christine Dietzel 10/17/78–11/29/96
Margaret K. Mitter 9/9/21–8/3/99

For my sons,
Kevin and Soren

Let this book of the flowers hold the essence of my Being

Let it hold in its bind-
ings all of the passions
of my youth.
Let it harbor the birth
and renaissance of
my inspirations.
Let the dreams that
will inevitably fall
over the pages of
this book be blessed.
And lastly:
To they that find
themselves drawn to
this book ~ read it
with freedom and
let it be a joy to
you!

Opening page to Nina's journal, started September 1995

Contents

Preface XII

Part I

At the Threshold
Exposed 2
Unbounded Joy 3

Connections
Family Friends 6
Camphill Village 9

Preparation
Community Life 17
Adolescence 34
High School 48
Seventeen 58
Mountain Magic 63
Goodbyes 71

Fulfillment
Eighteen 77
A Visit 81
Life in Harlemville 91
Thanksgiving Day 93
Thoughts of Nina 94

Part II

November 29, 1996

The Day after Thanksgiving in Golden Valley   98
The Accident   102
That First Night   106

November 30, 1996

Waiting   108
Arrival   112

December 1, 1996

Sunday Morning   116
Poetry, Art, and Music   120
Endless Day   124

December 2, 1996

Final Goodbye   128
Funeral   131

The Week in Harlemville

Nina's Room   135
Packing Away   139
On Nina's Desk   140
Nina's Journal   142
Numinous   146
Singing   147

Coming Home

In Shock   149
Advent Consolation   151
Days with Soren   152
Words of Consolation   154
Baby Steps   159
Linda's Homecoming   160

Memorial

Friends   162
Elegy   164
Gratitude   167
Christmas Candles and Roses   168
Ministered to by Angels   171

Dreams   173

Carrying On

Out of Seclusion   179
New Reality   185
Life Review and Reading   187
Where Two or Three are Gathered   190
Two of Us   193

Spring

She Would Draw Flowers   197
Caretaking   200
New Layers   202
May Day   203
Nina's Story   205

Summer

Pilgrimage   213
Journey Into Nina's Space   216
Profound Love   219
Nine Little Children   220
Cheesecake   222

Autumn

Room Switch   224
Melancholy   226
First Anniversary   231

Part III

Healings

Winter   236
Get-away   240
Stories   242
Another Birthday   246

At the Threshold

Thresholds Remembered   248
Departure   251
Last Visit   255
Final Farewell   257
Gathering In   259
Life Cycles   263
My Mother   264

Stories

New Freedom   267
Simple Joy   269
Three Years   273
Eternal Connection   276

Preface

The three years from 1996 to 1999 were the most turbulent years of my life. The sudden accidental death of my daughter, Nina, in the fall of 1996 was followed by the decline of my mother's health with Parkinson's disease until her passing in August of 1999.

When I began to write this book in the fall of 1999, I wanted to record the details surrounding Nina's accident before they became fuzzy. I thought my two sons, ages 15 and 4 when Nina died, might someday find themselves wondering what exactly had happened, and I wanted the facts clearly recorded in one place.

I also needed to take much-needed solitary time, once my youngest son was in school, to reflect on the sequence of events surrounding my double loss, and sort through the myriad emotions I was experiencing. Writing was a crucial part of my grief journey.

Ultimately, though, I wanted to find a way to express the wonder that I felt about my own life and all that had befallen me. While I was devastated by the loss of my child, I experienced a profound holiness that transcended the normal experiences of everyday life and changed me forever. Nina, from across the threshold, led me in the mission for this book. Many mornings I woke up with the words for the next section singing in my head. Inspiration for the title and vision of this book came to me long before I started writing.

I "finished" the book in the spring of 2000 and gave a reading to friends and family in August of that year.

Shortly thereafter, I moved with my family to Harlem-ville, New York, for nine months. I put the book aside while I walked in Nina's footsteps in this small rural community where she died, healing in a visceral way.

Upon our return to Minnesota, I was engaged for several years in forging my new identity after these life-altering events. This book floated in the background as I waited for the right connection to arise that would lead to its incarnation. When I met Nancy Manahan and Becky Bohan, authors of *Living Consciously, Dying Gracefully: A Journey with Cancer and Beyond*, in the spring of 2007, I found my connection. They graciously volunteered to edit my book. Over a period of almost two years, we sent sections back and forth to each other as time allowed; their gentle suggestions were followed by my rewrites, deletions and additions. What I had writ-ten years before provided only landmarks on the road map to those three transformative years; now I had to fill in the details to bring the events and characters to life. I am unceasingly grateful for their invaluable mentoring.

Going back to re-experience and describe my feel-ings from years ago took me through another phase of my grief journey. I went through a period of ques-tioning whether exposing myself and my family to the public in publishing this book was the right thing to do. I felt I might be criticized for dwelling on my loss of so long ago.

Overcoming this doubt was an empowering process. With it comes the hope that my story will help others to embrace their life stories, to periodically look back in order to shed new light on how their lives have moved forward, and to reflect on and honor the continued presence in their lives of deceased loved ones.

To you, dear reader, if you have lost a child, my wish is to offer hope for your own healing, as I have healed. To anyone else drawn to read this book, my wish is that my personal experience might shed light on our mutual experience as human beings coping with what comes to us in life. Each person brings to his or her earthly incarnation unique gifts and a path toward unfolding who they are to become.

Acceptance, love, and respect for the individual and the path they have chosen can give us strength to face the unexpected in the lives of our children, parents, brothers, sisters, and companions on this journey of life.

Marianne Dietzel
May 2010

Part I

At the Threshold

❧

Exposed

I never entertained the question of what I would do if I lost a child. Yet, on one November day in Minnesota, I had the fleeting thought, as I walked up the stairs from the basement to the main floor of our suburban 1950's rambler, that we led a charmed life. No one in my immediate or extended family had been involved in any serious accidents. How could we have escaped unscathed from the dangers of everyday existence?

A week later, walking up the same stairs, I still could not imagine that a loved one was in danger. It was the day after Thanksgiving, November 29, 1996. I had arrived home with our youngest son, Soren, after having taken our older son, Kevin, and two friends to Uptown in Minneapolis for the afternoon. My husband, Dennis, was coming down the stairs with the afghan draped around his shoulders and a haggard look on his face. He should have been at work.

He said, grimly, that Soren and I should come upstairs; he had something to tell us. All I could think of was that he had lost his job. But the look on his face told me it had to be something worse.

The following moments catapulted us into a new realm of existence. Nothing could hold us back from it. We were at the threshold, exposed naked to the heavenly worlds and to our community. Into this existence we brought all that we were: the influence of our family and upbringing, the twists and turns on our paths to adulthood and creating our own family, the spiritual life we had nurtured, the decisions we had made. We could change nothing now. There was no stopping for preparation. This was all we had to face the moment.

Our daughter Nina, her friend Kirsten, and Kirsten's mother Linda had been in a car accident. Linda was alive. Nina and Kirsten were dead.

Unbounded Joy

Our family lives in the city. This was not always so. We knew a different life, enmeshed in the cycles of the year on the land, whose bounty provided for the sustenance of body and spirit. Now, we fight traffic and schedules to scavenge for our daily bread. Our meals together give us a brief reprise and soulful nourishment, but all too often our activities drive some of us to our cars again before the others have barely arrived home.

Grief over all that we left behind in the country often simmers under the surface of our family dynamics. We find our deeper connections to each other and to life when we flee the city to be in nature together.

The second summer after Nina died was an empty

and desolate time. While inwardly experiencing transformation of our loss, we were in desperate need of
something to speak to us from the outer world, of finding it a safe place to live in again. Kevin, now 17, was
away on adventures of his own. With nothing calling
us to travel afar for our vacation, Dennis, Soren, and I
went on several camping trips in Minnesota. In August,
we drove over three hours to a state park on the north
shore of Lake Superior.

We set up our campsite and went out walking on the
huge rocks jutting out from the shore, watching the sunset over the lake. After a quick rainstorm, we returned
to the campsite and bedded down for a peaceful night in
our tent. We felt lucky to be in such a beautiful spot.

In the morning we got a different impression of our
campsite. Anytime we brought food out, bees descended
furiously, making it impossible to eat. We packed snacks
and lunch, put on swimsuits under our clothes, attached
fishing poles to our backpacks, and started hiking. We
were prepared for adventure.

We followed a trail to the river, and then lazily made
our way upstream, hopping from boulder to boulder.
After about two hours of this relaxed sort of hiking
(which six-year-old Soren loved), the boulders started
disappearing, so we followed the path along the side
of the river. Then we heard the roar of a waterfall. We
came upon it from above. It was not just one waterfall;
there were several cascades plunging down the enor-
mous boulders, here in a widespread fan, there in a
narrow channel.

We actually climbed *down* the boulders to the bottom

of the falls. And there we discovered a person-sized waterfall, reachable from the edge, with smooth boulders lining the bottom. We were warm enough that the water looked inviting. All we needed to do was take off our clothes. Something pulled me out of my normally cautious self, and when Dennis looked at me, I said, "I'm going to do it!"

When the three of us got under that pounding falls and looked up at the water heedlessly and endlessly falling down upon us, all we could do was laugh. All we could feel was joy. My husband, my son, and I laughed and laughed in that waterfall. And when we had enough, we returned to the edge and sat on the rocks in our bathing suits, quietly absorbing the warmth of the sun, letting the joy sink deep into our hearts.

We all knew that it was not just the three of us there. Another presence was wafting through the air, the light, the roar, the mist, permeating every cell of our beings. Dennis finally gave words to it: Nina was smiling down on us from the top of the waterfall.

No one else came to the waterfall. On our way back down the river, we only saw one family. Had other people been around, we could never have experienced the waterfall as we did. In those brief moments of unbounded joy, we felt securely surrounded by nature imbued with Spirit. Yes, it was still possible to find a place in the natural world that was sacred.

That affirmation filled me to overflowing. I knew that our shining spirit-child guided us to that waterfall, gave us the courage to cross the threshold, and helped us to feel again the joy of existence.

Connections

❧

Family Friends

Two little girls stand together in their kindergarten class photograph. Nina has blue eyes and a broad smile, her blond hair hangs gracefully to her shoulders. She is taller than all the rest, as she will be throughout grade school, and sturdily built. Kirsten, shorter and slighter, has thick dark brown hair with bangs and a bob down to her chin, and a red rosebud mouth. She is looking down, obviously preoccupied with something other than the photograph being taken.

Nina and Kirsten must have been attracted to each other back then, when they first met as five or six-year-olds. Nina's smooth white skin and light hair reflected her gentle, soft-spoken nature. She was often the one who was standing to the side watching the other children, waiting for familiarity to allow for spontaneity. Kirsten, on the other hand, was the exuberant one, quick to warm up and express herself. Was it the attraction of the opposite, of finding what one needed in the other, that drew them together?

Kirsten and Nina next to their Kindergarten teacher,
Mary Lou Bala

It certainly helped that Linda Bergh, her mother, and
I had a lot in common and soon became friends as well.
Both of our families had moved to the Twin Cities/
Minneapolis in 1983/84 so our children could attend
the Minnesota Waldorf School, one of the few Waldorf
schools in the Midwest. Paul, Linda, and Kirsten had
moved from California; Dennis, Nina, Kevin, and I from
Indiana. Both our families liked Waldorf's holistic and
artistic approach to education, which was reflected in
our home environments. We cooked with natural foods,
created toys from natural materials, observed the festivals tied to the seasons of nature, and minimized media
exposure. We chose hiking, biking, skiing, canoeing, and
camping for family recreation.

Nina and Kirsten started first grade together with a teacher who was to stay with them through eighth grade. I taught German at the school for a few years and Linda taught Kindergarten. Paul and Dennis served on the Board of the school a little later. At first, both families lived in the same neighborhood, near the school, and the girls often played at each others' houses. At our house, their creative play often involved Kevin, who was two years younger than Nina. Kirsten had no siblings, but had no problem accepting the presence of a "little brother"— in fact, sometimes having a little brother was all the more fun for playing house, playing school, or building forts and castles.

In 1985, we bought our first house a little further away. The Berghs came to our housewarming party that summer between the girls' first- and second-grade years. After that, our friendship as families flourished through Sunday-afternoon outings, shared meals, and weekend camping trips.

One spring, Paul introduced us to the rock cliffs and trout streams of Whitewater State Park. A native of southeastern Minnesota, he led us up the 300 stone steps to the ridge overlooking the Whitewater River Valley. The next winter, we were invited to the Bergh family cabin north of Grand Rapids. This was our introduction to the proverbial Minnesota "cabin up north" we had heard about. We chopped a hole through the ice on the lake to get drinking and washing water, observed the vast night sky in sub-zero temperatures, and cross-country skied through the pristine pine and birch forests.

Although Nina and Kirsten shared a special bond, they celebrated their birthdays with all the girls from their class. Kirsten's was in July, and her parties always included water, either by a lake or on the Slip 'N Slide in the backyard. Nina's was in October and was often marked by the visit of "Oma" (Nina's maternal grandmother), who was famous for making party hats, directing treasure hunts, and leading old-fashioned party games like Find the Thimble, Musical Chairs, and Button, Button, Who's Got the Button?

Camphill Village

The summer after Nina was in third grade our family made a radical move. We rented our house to some friends and moved to the country to live "in community." This was something Dennis and I had always talked about, but we had never been drawn to any particular community. When we visited Camphill Village Minnesota we were surprised to find a place that might be a home for us. It is a group of about 60 people who live on a farm two hours northwest of the Twin Cities. Here, people with and without developmental disabilities work together in a community reflecting the principles of anthroposophy, the philosophy also underlying Waldorf education. This was a place where our family life and values could be nurtured.

Dennis and I had embraced anthroposophy as a path of self-development. This included study of books and lecture cycles by Rudolf Steiner (Austrian philosopher, 1861–1925) and a personal practice of meditation.

Anthroposophy, meaning "the wisdom of the human being," emphasizes individual freedom in the quest for knowledge of the world beyond the senses. Spiritual practice is built upon the development of the whole human being in thinking, feeling, and willing.

Steiner's practical application of his philosophy in the fields of medicine, architecture, agriculture, and education was a compelling attraction for us. Here, in this intentional community, we had an opportunity to express our inner striving in our everyday activities with others also inspired by anthroposophy.

In addition, we had an opportunity to live on a farm, a dream long held by Dennis. We knew we were asking a lot of our children to leave their friends and teachers at the Waldorf School. We didn't know how it would work for us to share a house with others. We were willing to give it a try.

Camphill Village Minnesota (CVM) was established in 1980, one in a network of worldwide Camphill communities that were started in Scotland in 1939 by Austrian pediatrician Karl Koenig. In Camphill, individuals are seen in their essential humanness and find their place within the community, regardless of ability. This reputation led to an invitation by a group of parents to start a village in Minnesota.

In 1988, Camphill Village Minnesota was in a period of expansion. That summer, two other families with young children arrived at CVM. The Leighton family had two girls, Gwyneth and Annamaria, close to Nina's age, and a boy younger than Kevin. The Gammeter family had a boy, Christian, close to Kevin's age, and a younger girl. The children thrived with their new friends, in the freedom and safety of living close to nature, and with all the new activities that farm and community life provided.

Nina took the long bus ride into the nearest town, Long Prairie, to attend fourth grade in a parochial school. Kevin, in second grade, was home-schooled along with Christian and some of the younger children. This allowed him more time to absorb everything that was happening on the farm. He spent hours in the barn and barnyard watching the cows, chickens, and pigs, and the people working with them.

Nina, when she was home, didn't have the same intense interest in the farm, although she, Gwyneth, and Annamaria often passed through on their wanderings. They were more interested in each other, and totally immersed in the play of "the heart of childhood." At ages 10 and 12, they could carry through with activities of their own invention. They sewed doll clothes, styled each other's hair, and built elaborate forts in the woods.

Dennis and I had several roles in Camphill Village. First of all, we were house parents. Four adults with special needs, plus an experienced Camphill volunteer, George, lived with us. Evelyn, Brian, Erick, and Greg had their own bedrooms and we created a home environment for them. George, Dennis, and I oversaw their grooming, room cleaning, social lives, medical appointments, and communications with their families.

Every morning we got them off to their work assignments—Evelyn and Brian to the bakery and Erick and Greg to the farm—and every afternoon to the weavery, grounds crew, or woodshop. We had breakfast ready when Erick returned from milking the cows in the morning, a large meal at noon, fresh bakery bread at 4:30 for "tea time" before the evening milking, and a simple supper. It was a demanding schedule. It was a privilege and a challenge to share life with these open-hearted, vulnerable individuals.

I managed a crew of 2–3 people with disabilities who came to the house every morning to help with meal preparation, laundry, and cleaning. I did a weekly shopping run into Long Prairie. My one farm responsibility was feeding the chickens, collecting eggs, and cleaning the chicken coop, with Kevin as my helper. Dennis worked on the dairy farm nearly full time, helping with the milking and the field work. We both helped plan many of the festival celebrations and other cultural activities of the Village.

The routines and dynamics of our family life changed dramatically. With a two and a half gallon pail of fresh milk delivered to our house several times a week, making yogurt and butter became regular chores. We learned how to ask Greg to pass the honey and bread in sign language, and to understand Evelyn's "gibberish" when she told us stories of her parakeet and embroidery projects. Erick was now the dishwasher and Evelyn set the table, jobs which normally would have fallen to Nina and Kevin. Brian needed supervision for dressing, grooming and bathing, as a child younger than Nina and Kevin would.

With 9–12 people regularly at our breakfast, lunch, and supper table, family intimacy became scarce, mostly happening behind our bedroom doors at the end of

Our lunch table at Camphill Village Minnesota: Erick, Marianne, Brian, Killian, Dennis, Greg, Evelyn, Kevin and Nina

the hall on the second floor. Kevin and Nina shared a bedroom next to ours. Dennis and I had a large master bedroom with our own bathroom, which Nina and Kevin also used, and a small balcony with stairs to the back yard. Our bedroom had space for a couch, where we read bedtime stories and snuggled with our children. During the daily rest hour after lunch, we all had quiet time in our rooms, which often meant a nap for Dennis and me and reading by themselves or quiet playing for the kids.

We tried to continue some normal child-centered activities, but it was sometimes challenging. In October of that first year at Camphill Village, Nina invited all the girls from her city Waldorf School class to our new home for her tenth birthday. She was excited to share our new country lifestyle, complete with a hayride and dead gophers trapped by the farmers to inspect. Ten fourth-graders and ten sleeping bags managed to squeeze into our living room. Even though Nina was offended when I came in with my lyre at midnight to settle the girls down with some soothing music, the overnight was a success. The girls got up early enough that our household was able to go on functioning without too much disruption in the morning. It was an eye opener for Nina's friends to have breakfast with Evelyn, Brian, Erick, and Greg, and George, the new members of our family.

By the end of our "trial" year at Camphill Village we had raised a flock of laying hens from chicks, seen a few calves born, sent some pigs off to market, put on a Christmas play, baked a wedding cake, canned dozens of quarts of tomatoes, and learned a new repertoire of songs. We survived a drought, Erick running away, Greg having a violent temper tantrum at the breakfast table, and our cat devouring Evelyn's parakeet. It was now time to take stock.

During this year, I experienced a feeling of familiarity deep in my bones that did not relate to anything I knew in this life. I felt as though I had known and worked with these people in a time that memory couldn't touch. I felt this especially when everyone in the village walked the paths from their houses to gather in the central hall. In singing, listening to talks on spiritual subjects, folk dancing, or planning our weekly activities together, I found sustenance for the daily work I did as an individual, linking me to the whole. Camphill expressed some archetypal way of life that we in the modern world have lost touch with, not as an anachronism, but as a vital organism. One part of me resonated deeply with this intentional way of living.

Another part of me rebelled at the isolation and rigidity of its rhythms. There was little room for spontaneity. Going on a family picnic because the sun was shining was virtually impossible because we needed to plan in advance for house coverage. Participation in activities in the surrounding community was limited for the same reasons. Rituals, such as a morning circle after breakfast, gave stability to the folks with special needs, and built patience and discipline in us, but this regimen tied us down. It was not easy for a modern family to adapt to a life based on commitment to others.

After weeks of deliberations Dennis and I decided to move our family back to the city. We needed to get some distance and see what life was like as a nuclear family again. New houseparents took over caring for Evelyn, Brian, Erick, and Greg. Our Twin Cities tenants found a house to rent across the street and, by August 1989, we were back home.

Nina and Kevin rejoined the Minnesota Waldorf School, she for fifth grade, he for third grade. The children missed the closeness of their Camphill friends, but were able to blend easily into familiar surroundings and the richness of Waldorf education.

Nina and Kirsten happily resumed their friendship. Their activities now were flavored with typical pre-adolescent culture, but Nina and Kirsten still loved accumulating wardrobes for their "Kirsten" dolls (from the American Girls Collection). They also loved watching

"Anne of Green Gables" videos during overnights at the Berghs. Paul and Linda had purchased a new house in the Linden Hills area with Patrick and Diana O'Brien. Paul, Linda, and Kirsten lived upstairs, while Patrick, Diana, and their daughter Molly (Kevin's age) lived downstairs. Molly became a third in the friendship when Nina visited Kirsten.

That next year was difficult for Dennis and me. Dennis went back to his job as a computer programmer at Schroeder Milk Company. I did some temporary office work and public school substitute teaching. I thought about becoming a class teacher at the Waldorf School the next fall. In the spring, we helped start a community garden in Osceola, Wisconsin, on the weekends, but it wasn't very workable to have to drive so far to garden. We were not sure where we fit. There were so many aspects of life at Camphill that we loved and missed: the rich cultural life, including singing and festival celebration, and farm life in its abundance and simplicity.

After months of exploring other options, we decided that Camphill was where our ideals, our heart connections, and our work lay. Our children accepted this decision. They had good friends in both situations, so although it was hard to again leave one set, they got other friends back. From their perspective, Camphill was idyllic. This time we committed ourselves to a permanent move. We put our house on the market and took a family vacation to Yellowstone National Park in July of 1990. By the time we returned home, the house was sold. We packed up and moved back to Camphill Village in August.

Preparation

Community Life

The decision to return to Camphill involved home-schooling children in the Village. Some of the parents wanted to provide Waldorf education, which wasn't available locally. Several other parents and I had Waldorf teaching background. We cooperated in trying to give the children a homeopathic dose of what they might be getting in a proper Waldorf school.

The first year we returned to Camphill, we lived in a small house that did not include people with special needs. I concentrated my activities on the home-schooling endeavor, while Dennis managed the beef herd located on the Marlspring Farm adjoining the main 360 acres of the dairy farm. Our house, Marlspring, was on this property. The next year we moved into the neighboring house, Brome, when the house parents moved away. We then lived with three people with special needs, Paul, Jimmy, and David.

There were 6–8 children, ages 8–14, who were being home-schooled. We divided them into two groups according to age. These two groups had their main academic work in the mornings. Rooms were found in the common buildings to hold tables or desks and chairs. "Main lesson blocks" for several weeks at a time were rotated between the parents/teachers to cover developmentally-appropriate curriculum, such as Roman history, geography, fables and legends, Greek myths, botany, grammar, or geometry. From the teachers' presentations, the students created "main lesson books," with dictation, reports, essays, and illustrations.

Others in the Village taught the extra subjects they had expertise in, such as painting, handwork (knitting, crocheting, weaving, felting, sewing, etc.), woodwork, nutrition, cooking, movement, and music. David Leighton, Gwyneth and Annamaria's father, and I were main lesson block teachers. Dennis directed the Camphill Village orchestra, which included a mix of children and adults playing recorders, violin, viola, cello, and rhythm instruments. Lois Smith, the person who prepared the music for Village events, included the older children in the village choir, and Debbie, Gwyneth and Annamaria's mother, included children in plays she wrote and/or directed. Each week one of the parents drove the older children to St. Cloud, the nearest city, 50 miles southeast, for music lessons and shopping.

Nina, who turned twelve the fall we returned to the Village, thrived in this environment. The informal atmosphere of the "classroom" with her two best friends, Gwyneth and Annamaria, as classmates allowed for maximum engagement in the subjects. She loved the artistic work, playing viola in the orchestra, singing for

Kevin (cello) and Nina (viola) in the village orchestra with Dennis conducting

festivals, acting in a scene from Antigone, and spinning wool to knit a pair of homespun mittens.

Camphill Village was an ideal setting for home-schooling in many ways. Community life offered resources beyond the family, and a built-in structure to the days, weeks, and year based upon celebration of the seasonal festivals in a multi-dimensional way. Including the children in this life benefited both the children and the community.

The Advent season, four weeks leading up to Christmas, was especially filled with rituals that the girls loved. The Advent Garden took place on the first Sunday of Advent. Parents filled the Festival Hall with a spiral of evergreens on the floor ahead of time. When families arrived at dusk, they sat around the sides while musicians played and sang. Each child took a turn walking with a candle in an apple through the path between the evergreen boughs to the center candle, lit their small candle, and returned on the path, setting his/her apple down along the way. The evergreen spiral became a fragrant and glowing garden.

Annamaria recently told me that during one Advent season, Gwyneth, Nina, and she were asked to sing at the Advent Garden and light the center candle, dressed as angels. "We were meant to sing 'Ever Again Upon the Earth.' It was dead silent and we were so nervous. Gwyneth started doing a nervous swallowing/gulping thing and Nina and I burst out laughing and then we were all laughing. I'm sure you remember it, too. Wasn't it you who rescued us by starting the song?"

On December 13, Nina, Gwyneth, and Annamaria, as the eldest girls in the village, woke before dawn to dress as Santa Lucia and her attendants, all in white gowns. Debbie drove them around the village and re-lit the crown of candles on Santa Lucia's head at each house. The girls visited every person's room, waking them from sleep with a lovely song, serving sweet tea and cardamom-scented Santa Lucia bread. Many individuals remembered this as if angels appeared to them in a dream.

Soon after we moved into Marlspring, our family was initiated into farm life. The cows got out of their fenced area several times and all four of us pulled ourselves out of bed just after we had gone to sleep, or in the wee morning hours, to go outside to round them up.

Dennis soon figured out how to keep them where they belonged.

In the spring of that first year, we were surprised to have a "bottle lamb" delivered one Sunday morning by a sheep-farmer friend who had heard that Kevin was interested in an animal of his own. The whole family got involved in raising and training the lamb Kevin called Hector (until we found out it was a girl and she became Hectorina).

Nina wasn't interested in having animals. She loved spending her free time with Gwyneth and Annamaria. The threesome had a nursery rhyme to characterize themselves:

> "To bed, to bed, says Sleepy Head (Annamaria)
> Tarry awhile, says Slow (Nina)
> Put on the pan, says greedy Nan (Gwyneth)
> We'll sup before we go."

This refers directly to their bedtime habit of cooking up a snack before they parted. Annamaria reminisces, "We always made noodles with butter and salt and pepper, no marinara, and we would eat it straight out of the pot, each with our own fork. It was always late, so the house was quiet and it always felt cozy, just us in the lighted kitchen with the smell of butter and noodles." It also characterizes their relationship to each other: Annamaria and Gwyneth had their contrasting styles and temperaments, and Nina, simply through her calm and accepting presence, moderated the clashes that could occur between the two sisters.

Nina reached her full height, 5'8", and shoe size 10,

Nina in March 1991 (age 12)

by the end of sixth grade. She had the curves of a young woman, without the lankiness which characterized Gwyneth and Annamaria at this time. She was sturdy, with wide feet and hands. With her fine, silky, dishwater blond hair falling beneath her shoulders, fair complexion and full voluptuous lips, Nina had a Scandinavian-style gentle beauty. She elected not to have cosmetic orthodontia for the separation between her top two front teeth. When she put care into her appearance, she could look stunningly beautiful and older than her age. Most of the time during the next few years, however, she didn't give much attention to grooming, and I had to urge her to take showers more often. As each year went by, even though she wasn't growing taller, she added a few pounds, and her face became fleshier, her body full-figured.

Annamaria, who was Nina's age, had thick, coarse, blond hair the same color as Nina's. With her dark eyebrows and hazel eyes, she had a big-eyed fawn look. She was shy and introverted with the melancholy of an artist. Annamaria did not learn to read very easily, and Nina started reading to her the first year we were at Camphill. They continued this favorite pastime even as they got older, with lots of L.M. Montgomery, *The Riddle of Penncroft Farm*, *The Root Cellar*, and other young adult books.

Gwyneth, two years older, with dark strawberry blond hair, green eyes, a strong jaw line, and big smile, had a fiery temperament. She designed and sewed clothing and knit patterned sweaters with ease. Nina was a willing partner in scheming and carrying out many activities with Gwyneth. To Annamaria, Gwyneth seemed "bossy," while Nina loved the warmth of the companionship and busyness this friendship created, happily doing what Gwyneth suggested.

These three friends developed a relaxed and eclectic style of dressing, often wearing loose pants in flamboyant fabrics they had sewn themselves and cotton India shirts ordered from catalogs, or over-sized t-shirts. They prided themselves on not looking like the "teeny boppers" in town.

The whole village—six houses and farm buildings surrounded by woods, fields, and dirt roads—was the world for Nina, Gwyneth, and Annamaria. It offered opportunities to interact with individuals with developmental disabilities informally or in common projects, to care for and play with small children/babies, as well as to hang out with young volunteers (college age and beyond) from throughout the U.S. and Europe.

There was also a built-in clientele for entrepreneurial activities. For a December Advent Fair, the three girls made felt finger puppets and gnomes, Advent calendars, beaded jewelry, and scherenschnitte (cut paper) bookmarks to sell. One spring evening they cooked cream of carrot soup, cheese and onion quiche, and a mixed-green salad for a village cafe. On hot summer days, they sold spritzers and chips on a wagon set up by the path where people would pass on their way home from work.

For outdoor adventures, the three girls banded together with the boys close to their age, including both younger brothers, Kevin Dietzel and Ciaran Leighton. Riding Lucky the pig was a favorite activity. Gwyneth recalls, "It was such a thrill, to creep slowly up to a pig, jump on its back, and cling for dear life as it tore across the yard, terrified and squealing. We tried to see who could stay on the longest—it was never more than a few seconds, really, but we split our sides laughing at the sight!" They played in the hayloft and explored a hidden wooded island in the marsh. Each spring they made a ritual "first swim" in the nearby Sauk River, jumping in from the rope swing.

Nina kept up with several of her friends from Minneapolis, inviting them to spend a weekend at different times. Kirsten and Nina continued celebrating their birthdays together whenever they could. We drove Nina to the Bergh's cabin for two years. In October of 1991, Kirsten came to the Village to join Nina, Gwyneth, and Annamaria for a party to celebrate Nina's turning 13.

That fall, as Dennis and I began parenting a teenager, a surprise pregnancy catapulted us in the opposite direction. This baby would be a "second chapter," as my Aunt Becky called it. Once Dennis and I got over the surprise and shared this news with our children and the Village, we enjoyed this pregnancy in a very different way than the first two. It was physically more difficult, but our experience and age allowed us to go through it with less anxiety. Nina was overjoyed, for she had always wished for another sibling. Ten-year-old Kevin had no objections, but didn't show the same interest.

One Saturday in November, Dennis and I accompanied several of the older children of the Village (including Nina) to the Guthrie Theater in Minneapolis to see Shakespeare's *The Tempest*. Whom should we meet at the theater but Paul, Linda, and Kirsten Bergh! Although we visited with them during the intermission, it was too brief to share our delicate news. After this morning matinee, our Camphill Village group went out for lunch, then to Seven Corners where the girls wanted to shop. There, walking down the sidewalk, were the Berghs again! This time I told them the news of my pregnancy. They reacted with gasps and joyous laughter at the thought of another little Dietzel joining our almost-grown family.

Our dear little Soren was born in the early morning hours of June 20, 1992. I was forty years old, and feeling again the joys of motherhood. Of our three home births, this one went the most smoothly. What could be more perfect than having our good friend, a midwife, come at midnight from just across the road to attend the birth? Nina woke and was present for the last hour of labor. Kevin had to be awakened so that he wouldn't miss the grand finale. After the birth and in the following days, Nina held Soren and gazed at him as if he were her own. Kevin, much to my chagrin, went out to play in the woods the next day without even poking his head in on Soren and me. He needed encouragement to nurture a relationship with a baby.

We were interested in having Soren christened in The Christian Community, a denomination founded as a movement for religious renewal in 1922 inspired by Rudolf Steiner. Greg Brewer, the father of a community member, and a Christian Community priest, was visiting from Chicago for one remaining week and was available to conduct services and perform sacraments. It was not customary in this church to christen a baby only a week old (usually it happens at six weeks), nor was it customary to baptize 11 and 13-year-olds, but we had not had an opportunity to have Nina and Kevin christened when they were babies. Greg was willing to perform this sacrament for all three of our children that week. We began planning and choosing three sets of godparents.

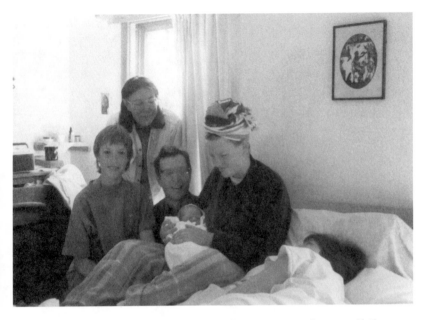

Marianne rests after giving birth to Soren at home, while Nurse-Midwife Mary Louise, Kevin, Dennis, and Nina admire the new baby.

Our dear friend, Laura Summer, who became a friend of the family in Minneapolis but now lived in an anthroposophical community in upstate New York, was already acting as Nina and Kevin's godmother. From our pool of friends from far and near, we chose the other godparents. The web of destiny became evermore entwined when we asked Paul Bergh to be Nina's godfather, and Linda Bergh to be Soren's godmother.

To the grand event of the christening, the Dietzel grandparents and all the godparents, except Laura Summer, were able to come. The Berghs arrived early on Sunday morning, June 28, to meet Soren and help get ready.

Nina holds Soren, a few days old.

Linda and Kirsten hold Soren dressed for his christening.

Kirsten was just about as excited as Nina over Soren, and loved getting him dressed in the long white christening gown borrowed from another Camphill family.

Under any other conditions, I would not have been able to have a christening so early, having barely recovered from childbirth. With Soren only a week old, the event was possible because the drive for mama and baby was only half a mile to the festival hall on the other side of the Village.

The service was short, but momentous. Nina and Kevin stood with their godparents and reverently took it all in. Dennis and I, so proud of our family, held our tiny newborn. I didn't shed a tear until the end of the ceremony, when the enormity of the occasion hit me, and I couldn't hold back a few gulping sobs.

The outdoor reception at our house was informal. We had a beautiful summer fruit salad in a watermelon basket and other salads, bread, and cheese out on the picnic table. People came to meet our guests and give cards, gifts, and congratulations to our three newly-christened children. After an hour, Nina and Kevin changed their clothes and escaped with their friends for a swim in the Marlspring pond.

The next week, in a rare moment of solitude for a new mother, I sat in a warm, soothing bath and sobbed in relief, exhaustion, and joy for all that I had been through, physically and emotionally.

The next year, Nina, now 14, decided to prepare for her confirmation in the Christian Community along with Annamaria. Greg Brewer, whose congregation was in Chicago, mailed Nina six lessons. Over the next few months, Nina and I read them together on Sunday mornings. Although they were beautiful, a deeper look into the seven "signs" in the Gospel of St. John and how they relate to the seven sacraments, I was not sure what they meant to Nina. We put them away for future reference.

Nina worked on sewing a dress for her confirmation with Kristen Wilson, another Camphill houseparent (one of the advantages of community living—there are other "mothers" to help with motherly duties). It was a cream colored, high-waisted peasant dress with a contrasting green bodice, true to her "folksy" style. She was proud of her accomplishment, gracefully executed with the help of Kristen's skill and creativity.

In April, Dennis and Debbie Leighton drove with the girls to Chicago for the actual confirmation. There they joined six other confirmands from the Chicago area for some preparation the night before the service and reception on Sunday morning. Nina seemed to be satisfied with the whole experience. She received thoughtful gifts from her grandparents and godparents, including a cloth-bound journal from her godfather, Paul. Kirsten kept a journal and probably helped her father come up with the idea, knowing that Nina did not have one.

I searched for just the right gift, one that had spiritual meaning. In June, Kirsten graduated from the eighth grade of the Minnesota Waldorf School. I later saw the program, and was touched by the Rudolf Steiner verse in it. I printed this verse for Nina on a fold-up paper star that could be hung by a ribbon. It seemed appropriate for a child becoming an adult, giving a hint of purpose in life to strive toward.

Nina and her godparents, Jan Zuzalek (for Laura Summer),
and Paul Bergh at her christening, June 28, 1992.

Kevin and Nina with Dennis and his parents at reception
on Marlspring Farm.

Annamaria and Nina at their confirmation, April 1993

May wisdom shine through me,
May love glow in me,
May strength penetrate me,
That in me may arise a helper of human kind,
A servant of holy things, selfless and true.

When I came upon this verse after Nina died, I found
it expressed the wonder I felt at the mystery of Nina's
short life and the holy purpose it served. I had a friend
copy it in calligraphy to have on display at Nina's memorial service.

Adolescence

The next year, 1993–94, was the last that we lived at Camphill Village. Having a baby/toddler, home-schooling children, and managing a Camphill house with three adults with disabilities was too stressful for me. Dennis and I also felt the conflict between personal needs and Village needs. We decided to take a year to make a careful exploration of the places where we might next live and work.

Dennis started transitioning out of farming, and trained a new young coworker to take on the beef herd. He spent at least half his time doing administrative work in the office. I started a pre-school, using the empty Marlspring House, for a few children of the Village and from neighboring families. It was challenging for me to do this with no colleagues to work with. I longed to be in the mainstream of Waldorf education; I was tired of the isolation in Long Prairie.

We asked Kevin and Nina to attend public school during this transition year to eliminate the stress of home-schooling. We thought public school was more appropriate for Nina as she began high school. Since her two dear friends, Gwyneth and Annamaria, would continue home-schooling, this was very difficult for Nina.

Kevin's home-schooling partner in the sixth grade, Nic, also decided to attend public school for his seventh grade year. Although the two friends did not attend the same school because their homes were in different school districts, Kevin did not take it as hard. He had attended public school for 5th grade and was in 4-H, so he knew some students.

Nina dutifully rode the bus 50 minutes to and from school in Long Prairie every day that year, endured the classes, did her homework, but wasn't really engaged. Her social life began when she came back home to the Village.

She was determined to accompany Gwyneth, Anna-maria, two other friends, and their teacher on a minivan journey to the Grand Canyon in the spring. Nina went to great lengths to arrange with her teachers to miss two weeks of school. This meant going in early and staying late to complete an exercise requirement for her physical education class. Humiliating and ridiculous as these workouts were, it was worth it to be with her friends on the trip, bonding further with them through the wilderness experiences they would have.

When they returned from the Grand Canyon, the three girls, two boys, and their teacher gave a dramatic outdoor presentation about their trip. Community members gathered on a hill by the Sauk River that flows through the Village property. The six travelers appeared from the bushes by the river, each of them covered from head to toe in mud. Standing in a circle, they read their essays about memorable moments of the trip, sang a few songs, and then let out a whoop, dove into the river, and swam away. It was clear to all of us witnessing this drama that they had experienced transformation on their journey. With this exposition before the community, they completed their rite of passage.

Overshadowing the whole year was the imminent

move. Nina wrote to my sister-in-law Andrea on January 16, 1994, about her life at Camphill:

Right now, I'm extremely happy yet in the same moment I'm so confused. I am constantly wondering about the future and the upcoming year and what it has to bring us, yet I also dread this June when we must pack up our life here and leave these dear people and places. Gwyneth, Annamaria, and I will be, and are being hit extremely hard with separating after being and living almost as one for the last four years. This is really as though we're all turning to a new chapter in life to seek out a new life of different people and places. They are each going to a year of school in Vancouver and Ireland to attend Waldorf schools. I was telling another friend that when we moved from Minneapolis it was as though my spirit was born anew. Here I developed who I am, my true being, my foundation for life. It was here that all my dreams and expectations for life were born. Though I'm sure I will be happy wherever we turn up, I often wonder why this particular good life can't go on how it is!

The Bergh family spent this year in France, a dream come true for them. Paul and Linda taught in a Waldorf boarding school and Kirsten repeated the eighth grade, completely immersed in French. Kirsten invited Nina to visit in the summer. Nina and Kirsten corresponded about this, but Nina also talked about the Farm and Wilderness (F & W) camp called Saltash Mountain (SAM) in Vermont she went to the summer before ninth grade. The Farm and Wilderness camps, which I attended as a child, have a unique Quaker-influenced philosophy which Nina appreciated, as I did.

11.15.93

My dearest Kirsten!
How fairest thou my little missy? It was so wonderful to hear from you, but what the hell, I received your letter, postmarked August 30, on November 1! What is the deal, did they decide to send it by ship? I feel really dreadful for not writing before, but I'll try and make that up with a really packy letter now!

From the sounds of your letter you need a cheery, uplifting letter, which I will try and fulfill. Whenever you're feeling down, just be glad that you're not going to the Long Prairie Public School, it is quite an ordeal!

Kirsten, my life is so packed with things happening, I want to tell you everything, feelings, thoughts, incidents, but I fear that will make a rather painful job for you, the reader! But nevertheless, here's a go of it!

Going to school is quite the thing, the most dreadful, but probably one of the best things I've ever done in life (besides, of course, going to camp this summer, which I'll tell you about later on). Some days I can hardly manage to roll out of bed just to hop on the bus to go to school, but most of the time, odd as it may seem, my spirit soars. It's not what happens at school but just being different and free in spirit makes me so happy. Everyone in school is your typical teenybopper with the strong Minnesota accent that drives all hell at me but also makes me burst out laughing. Somehow, to wear Birkenstocks and bellbottoms, eat whole wheat bread and say really off the wall kinds of things is really nice. I think that I'm probably the talk of everyone but as they always say, we give them something to talk about! The work is not all that challenging and I sometimes wonder whether there is any point in going, am I learning? I've adopted the nickname among some of "Tea Leaf." I don't know if I ever told you about the days when we smoked tea leaves, but they all were very eager to know if the new girl had ever smoked, so that's what I told them and thus, I am Tea Leaf. There are many really funny moments that I could fill this letter with, but the best is that someone thought I was Czech and spread it around, such strange notions people do get into their silly heads. Of course, it is definitely not all strawberries and cream and I spend too many depressing hours thinking of better days.

Better days. . . . A group of about twenty sleepy people gathered in the rough form of a circle holding hands, happily singing, feeling the dewy grass and the first rays of sunshine on their bare heads and feet. These were better days that I long for every moment of this real world we're living in. What I have described is a typical morning circle at Farm and Wilderness (the camp I went to). This simple but beautiful life is what we paid $2000 for but too worth it was it. Some of the best, most enriching and fulfilling days of my life come about here. This is partly (the truth, you must see and understand what this place means to me) the reason that I'm giving up ideas for France. It will be so hard for you to truly understand on paper, but try I will to make you see.

Up until about a week ago I thought it was pretty

*positive that I would come to see you in France, but then,
to throw off all plans, a close friend from camp called
and transported me back to SAM and I knew I had to go
back. To get there, the camp will help me pay so I only
have to give about $500. There is no other time in which
I can go back. Ages are up to 15 and I'll be pushing it
already, but I need it. Though there will also be no other
time for me to visit y'all folks in France, there is nothing really calling me to France save your beautiful self. I
truly feel that I'm doing the right thing and have strong
feelings also that our bond can last through this and that
we'll have a gorgeous reunion sometime in the next year
and it will be as though we never left.*

*As I'm sure I already told you, our family has to
MOVE next year and it's making me in a really foul
mood. Where? They won't decide! When? "Oh, sometime
in June, July or maybe August." (That sweet little phrase
was meant to be in my dad's voice!) Maybe Pennsylvania,
Minneapolis, St. Cloud, New York, the dear Lord knows!
As you can tell, that's a rather sore spot with me because
I don't have any friends anywhere but here in dear
Minnesota!*

*Well, my love, send photos, write letters, think
thoughts, and live life beautifully! Though life seems
so pointless sometimes, our little (or sometimes rather
elaborate) dreams of life are always hovering there to be
made true! Keep this in mind always and I love you more
than you know, sweetest!*

Your loving friends as Always,
Ninly

11.26.93

My precious Nin,

I thank you profusely for your letter, it affected me so much. I feel so terrible that I haven't written to you since August! Please find it in your heart to forgive me. In your letter, you said that I might be unhappy or angry when I read your letter, but it had the totally opposite affect on me; my heart hurt when I heard of your troubles, and my soul soared with yours when I read of your triumphs. Nina, I miss you so much, you could never imagine how much. Please don't take this the wrong way, I have tons of friends here, and adore my new(er) life here, but I often long for you and my other friends back there in lovely little Minnesota. First I'll write about the stuff in your letter, and then I will tell you a bit about my life here. I'm so glad that even though you don't seem to enjoy going to school you still maintain your regular self and behavior. It doesn't seem that the kids at your school are very nice, am I wrong? I hope that you do have some friends. Don't ever forget that you'll always have a friend with me around. Oh, Nin, don't feel so bad about not being able to come to France, I understand perfectly how much you love your camp and wilderness thing. I would probably do the same thing too.

Nin, listen to me, and follow my advice, I am literally begging you, if your family moves, my heart will shatter into billions of little pieces. I'm sure that it will eventually mend, but a huge gap in my mind and heart will be there forever. That is, if you move out of the state. I'll be just great if you move to another location in Minnesota, but will you be content there? I thought that you loved

*Camphill. Am I wrong? Anyways, I wish you the best of
luck deciding.*

   Your French (American) friend,
   Kirsten S. Bergh

February '94 (but I'm sending it in April!)
Dear Kirsten,
*Many warm greetings to you my French friend! My great-
est apologies for the great delay in this letter getting to
you. My motto, whether I like it or not, seems to be "few
and far between." You're not the only one who is getting
gypped in letters, so don't feel alone! Well, how is it all
trucking along? We out here in the boonies are trucking
beautifully along with hoards upon piles of snow and
chilly temperatures. I thank you so much for your two
gorgeous letters, it is lovely to hear it all and most tempt-
ing to just pop over and see you in the flesh. But, alack
and alas, it costs $ upon $ to get over there!*

   *I am absolutely dying to share with you my extreme
joy in living on the earth, but it is so hard to share,
meaning that I can't express to you on paper how I
feel. My spirit soars with the wind, dancing gleefully
to heights our earthly bodies can never reach, bringing
into me a surging rush of joy. It is most unexpressive, I
feel as though I must run in the wind, free of the bur-
dens of everyday life, to sing and dance, to hug all of my
dear friends and bring them into my beautiful world of
meadows, sunshine, thunderstorms, barefooted people,
gardens and other such pleasures.*

   *I'm free at times like this; there is nothing, which
can weigh down my spirit into the depths of earthly*

depressions and all of the other things, which are so typical of human beings. Why must we all, for the better time of our lives, fret and worry over money, looks, clothing and other equally silly things? It does absolutely no earthly good and I hope and wish that I could achieve in my life to avoid such pits. I have many frustrating times of pondering adults and what causes them to become who they are in their old age. Why must the youthful carefree spirits all be lost in the process of aging? This is my most frustrating subject and it is most bothersome to know that all of the beautiful, happy children must be drawn into this dark pit. I know that it is not all like this but that is the general image one gets from the masses.

If you find my letter, when I go on like this, rather pointless to read you must know that I have a different reason for writing letters than most. I could never sit down and write my mind down. I must have a purpose, so all of my mind is packed into envelopes and sent around the world to be read by my friends. I don't consciously say to myself that this is what I'm doing, I just recently found this to be true. So you see, whenever I need to express myself I sit down and write a letter.

The current situation is truly a lovely one. We are having so many really nice times together lately, meaning the Village crowd. Life here with good friends, surrounded by good people, good things, in a haven of love, warmth and friendship is so fulfilling. Though I go to school that does not count as part of my life. Life truly begins when I come home, slip into my overalls and let go of everything. This, of course, is what I would like it to be like, but it does not always work! This last four months of our existence in

*Camphill seems so powerful, so much will happen and I
will cherish every last minute of it.*

*Well, doll, I'll be saying cheerio now, I do love you
much and wish you much luck in something happening
with your French romance! I will be seeing you this summer, right? Much joy and glee I do wish into your life.*

Buckets of Sweet Love in a Basket,
Nina

June '94
"All My Lovin'"
*I just happen to be listening to the Beatles right now! My
mom's sending your mom a letter, so I decided to note
some things down to you.*

*Thanks so much for the letter, I think I got it the day
after I sent yours! I so hope you go to Southwest (High
School). Even if you don't we'll still be in the same town.*

*Nina, I can't tell you how much your letter (is that all
I can call it?) affected me. You're that kind of person that
the world needs more of; someone who can be different,
knows what she wants, can be so happy that her eyes
shine like stars and she seems to float on the fields of daffodils. It's harder for me to write like you did, but trust me
love, I have so many sweet times like that too.*

*Just a few minutes ago, I was walking back from
school, I felt like singing, dancing. . . . All of a sudden a
dog started to bark at me then another and then a whole
chorus of canines poured out their hearts to me (that's
how I saw it!), I just started to talk to them then, and
they got so frustrated, so loud, all the neighbors looked
out of their windows at me in astonishment! Then, my*

nose buried in a lilac, purple to say more, and all these old memories of Yesterday came flooding into my head. How life is good, how it changes. Changes are good, sometimes hard to adjust to, but necessary.

Strawberry fields forever

I'd much rather be high on life, drunk on the fluffy forms of clouds, intoxicated by the first sight of the peachy rose petals and their fuzzy feel. Do you catch my drift?

Listen babe, I'm gonna leave you now, get on with my homework.

Greet your conscience and your spirit for me please. Also, don't forget to write.

Love ya lots,

Kirsten S. Bergh

These letters reveal Nina and Kirsten's loyal friendship and youthful idealism. In spite of the years they lived apart, an endearing connection flourished through their correspondence.

The day Nina finished ninth grade, she shaved her head. Annamaria had done it a few weeks earlier, and Nina had asked me at that time if I would mind if she shaved her head, also. I discouraged her, but did not forbid her to do it. She respected this opinion, and then at the end of school came and asked me again. All I could think of was going to church in Fort Wayne, Indiana, when we would be visiting Dennis' parents in a few weeks. Again, I told her I was not fond of the idea, but I wouldn't stop her from doing it. She did. This was the final "good riddance!" to life in conservative Long

Prairie, and, like the "do-it-yourself" ear piercing she
had done with Gwyneth and Annamaria a few years
earlier, a slightly rebellious way to bond with her friends.
But what revealed her true nature was that she did not
want to cause any ill will with her rebellion. I admired
and loved her for daring to express her individuality.
Dennis admired the beautiful shape of her head that was
now exposed to view.

With this dramatic ending to the Camphill chapter
of Nina's life, she went off to Saltash Mountain Camp in
July of 1994 while we packed up our household to move
to the Twin Cities.

Nina wrote to Gwyneth back in the Village.

*Gwyneth, it was so wonderful to read your dear words
that I sat down and cried. I began to think that no matter where I am I have never experienced such a dear
friendship as yours. I was wondering if as time goes on I
will find others that I am able to experience this with.*

*Yes, I am here having a joyous time. At times I can
totally get sucked into this F & W world, this community
and this way of life, but then I remember my other world
which is so dear to me. Camphill is definitely something
with such a character of its own and I want to know this
way all of my life. You see what I mean don't you? No
matter where I really do turn out I want to integrate it
into my life if that is possible.*

The awareness and depth of soul that these teenage girls had is staggering. The letters have assured
me that, in spite of the changes our children endured,

Nina with a shaved head, summer 1994

Gwyneth, summer 1994

Nina and Annamaria with Lucia Leighton, summer 1994

we apparently provided them with fertile ground for healthy and creative development during adolescence.

High School

The indecision over where to live went on for a long time. Dennis searched for opportunities related to farming, but none of those worked out. Somewhat reluctantly, he accepted a job as administrator at the City of Lakes Waldorf School in Minneapolis. This job would provide the income to get a mortgage on a small fixer-upper house in Golden Valley (a northwest suburb of Minneapolis). As volunteers at Camphill, we had no savings beyond what was left from selling our house in south Minneapolis four years earlier.

At the last minute, the Waldorf school job fell through. Either Dennis would have to do computer work for the company he had worked with before, or we would have to back out of buying the Golden Valley house. We had moved our belongings out of Brome House to open it up for the family who was taking our place, and were temporarily living with our three children next door in Marlspring House with boxes waiting to be loaded onto the truck. What a crisis. We weren't in the right place, but we weren't moving to the right place either. We looked at drastic alternatives, like finding a job and renting a house in Long Prairie, and moving to a different Camphill. Nothing worked out. With strained emotions and painful compromises, Dennis and I signed the closing papers and moved to Golden Valley. Dennis returned to his computer work for Schroeder Milk Company.

The first years in Golden Valley were a strange mixture of ecstasy at the freedom of independent living, and mourning for the loss of community and rural life. Dennis felt the loss especially acutely with the drastic change from walking out the door to work on the farm, to commuting 14 miles to his office to sit and work at the computer for eight hours. Instead of coming home for a farmer's meal with a household of nine in the middle of the day, he ate a brown bag lunch alone at his desk in his windowless office.

In September of 1994, I started a half-time job as a kindergarten assistant at the Minnesota Waldorf School. I found Kim Pilgrim, a Waldorf mom with a 1-year-old close to our new house, to care for 2-year-old Soren in the mornings. Kim's daughter Rachael, coincidentally, was also Linda Bergh's godchild, although we didn't discover this until we met. This began a very close friendship with the Pilgrim family. Rachael and Soren became like siblings. Dennis gave Kim a break one morning a week and took off work himself to bake bread with the two little ones, a highlight in the week for parents and children.

Nina, now a sophomore, went to Robbinsdale-Armstrong High School, a mega-high school about five miles west of our house. Kirsten's family was back in Minneapolis, too. Kirsten was a year behind Nina because she had repeated eighth grade in France. The Berghs still lived in the upstairs of the house they shared with the O'Brien family in south Minneapolis. Although Kirsten went to a different high school, Nina had weekly viola lessons near her house, and they often got together after her lesson. There were other get-togethers, too, such as an October outing with the Berghs to Whitewater State Park in southeastern Minnesota, Molly O'Brien's birthday party in November, Advent singing at our home in December, and a spring outing to Nerstrand State Park in south-central Minnesota.

Not knowing anyone, Nina found her new suburban high school with 2,000 students daunting. Her social life began to bloom when she got into the winter school play, Antigone. Here she found people with similar interests who eventually welcomed her into their fold. She also joined Armstrong's declamation team. All of a sudden her days and weeks were busy. Along with these extracurricular activities, she was earning money babysitting and helping elderly neighbors with leaf raking, painting, and snow shoveling. She wanted to fund a trip to Ireland in the summer to visit Annamaria.

Before her summer trip, in March of 1995, Paul, Linda, Dennis, and I took a car trip to Chicago one weekend to see a play. Nina, Kevin, and Kirsten stayed at home with Soren. This was an unprecedented getaway for us, and we had a laughter filled time with Paul and Linda. On the car ride there, we listened, enthralled, to Paul's life story. This was a man so present in the moment, in current issues and ideas, and intent on having a good time that we never had heard about his past. We learned that he had suffered from rheumatic fever as a boy, which created a hole in a valve resulting in an enlarged heart. We remembered his two operations in the early 1980s, one to have a new valve put in, and one to perform a bypass.

In July, we sent Nina off on the airplane to Ireland,

with trepidation about our 16-year-old traveling alone
to Europe. Once there, however, she was within the
embrace of Annamaria and the Irish family with whom
she was living at Camphill Glencraig near Belfast.
Annamaria recalls one particular day "when we skipped
school and walked into the town of Holywood (where
the school is) along the Loch and then up into the hills.
We wandered around up there all day and at one point,
laid under a big tree in the middle of some pasture.
There Nina read *Tess of the D'urbervilles* to me, probably
half the book. I have the book still, and even though it is
the most depressing of stories, it reminds me so strongly
of that beautiful day spent with Nina."

Nina and Annamaria took a day trip to Dublin where
they went to Trinity College and saw The Book of Kells,
the illuminated Biblical manuscript from the early
Middle Ages and Ireland's finest national treasure. They
also traveled with the family to visit the Giant's Cause-
way on the northeast coast of Northern Ireland, an area
of majestic cliffs, hidden bays, 40,000 interlocking basalt
columns, and legends of shipwrecks.

Two weeks later, when we picked up Nina at the airport, we could tell by her saunter and smile that she was
pleased with herself. She had fulfilled a dream through
her own effort. But most of all, she had enjoyed a very
special time with one of her dearest friends.

Nina filled the remainder of her summer with
babysitting commitments, time with Kirsten, and visits
to Camphill. One night, while Nina was at Camphill,
Linda called to tell us that Paul had been taken to the
hospital. He had been running errands on his way home

from work when he started having trouble breathing. He asked someone to call an ambulance. By the time Linda arrived at the hospital, he was unable to speak or make eye contact. He could only squeeze her hand.

That night Paul went into cardiac arrest. When Kirsten reached the hospital, her father was unconscious.

This began a four day ordeal for Linda, Kirsten, and many friends. Dennis, deeply saddened by the sudden decline of one of his best friends, spent the next two evenings at the hospital, while I stayed home with Soren. The day after Nina returned from Camphill, she spent many hours with Kirsten in the hospital, supporting her friend in giving up hope that her father would live, and then finding ways to say goodbye to him. The hospital staff was awed by the continual presence of friends and family, talking, praying, and singing with Paul.

Because I was at home with Soren, I went to the hospital only once before he died. That experience of seeing my friends surrounded by hospital procedures, machines, and medical personnel was challenging. My only previous hospital experience was when my father had two strokes when I was 15. I felt sad when I realized Kirsten was only a year younger than I was at 17 when my father died. I sat with Kirsten in the family lounge after she had been singing with her father as her way to help him die.

I supported Linda, Paul, and Kirsten as best I could from home. I made phone calls for Linda. Other friends and I tried to find out all we could about keeping Paul's body at home for the wake. Linda wanted to keep this time more personal and honor the sacredness of the

first three days after death when, according to Rudolf
Steiner, the life forces are gradually leaving the physical
body and the soul experiences a panoramic view of the
life just ended.

Although none of us had ever needed the practical
details, we knew that we wanted to be more involved
than we would be if we turned Paul over to a funeral
home. I got what information I could from out-of-state
people I knew who had held a home vigil, and Patrick
O'Brien (Paul's housemate and very close friend) contacted cooperative funeral homes about the legal require-
ments in Minnesota.

Paul died Friday afternoon, August 4, 1995. Singing
accompanied him as he approached and crossed the
threshold.

That afternoon and during the next three days, our
advance phone calls made it possible to do things the way
Linda wanted. The Cremation Society transported Paul's
body to their facility. There, with the assistance of the
funeral director, Linda, Dennis and Diana O'Brien washed
and dressed him. Linda purchased a modest coffin from
the funeral home, and Paul was transported home in their
hearse. Linda and friends followed in the car.

Dennis and Patrick helped to carry the 250-pound Paul
in his coffin into the beautiful cedar meditation hut he
had built in his back yard. The hut was a 10' x 12' room
with the door, windows, and a porch along the north
side. Dennis and Patrick had to tip the coffin sideways
to get it in the door, and then rearrange Paul when they
placed the coffin on a gurney along the south wall. On the
shorter, west, wall, there was a little table adorned with

flowers, candles, and photos. Paul lay in state wearing the elegantly flashy black shirt and floral tie that he had worn to Nina's christening.

Earlier that Friday afternoon, after many phone calls, Dennis found a bait shop with enough dry ice to preserve Paul's body, which had not been embalmed. When he picked up the 50 pounds of ice, the two old women who ran the bait shop exclaimed, "You sure must have a lot of fish!"

Dennis and Patrick, wearing work gloves, tucked the chunks of dry ice in brown paper bags under Paul's lower back and along the sides of his body, concealing the ice with the silky blue cloth that lined the sides of the coffin. It was very hot that August, and there was no air conditioning in the hut, but this method of keeping his torso cool prevented unpleasant odors from arising. The dry ice eventually evaporated and had to be replenished each day. Another proprietor (an ice cream truck supplier) joked, "Wow, you must have a big body to keep cold!" Dennis did not tell him that yes, indeed, Paul was a big man.

Paul's three-day wake was an extraordinary community event. Many friends took turns sitting with Paul around the clock. Dennis courageously came for a midnight–2:00 AM shift. I was not so generous with my sleep time, nor brave enough to go out in the middle of the night and sit alone with a dead body. I preferred coming at 6:00 AM when it was light, but still quiet. This was a solitary time. I came armed with the Bible, a book of verses by Rudolf Steiner, and the Bhagavad Gita. Largely because of my experience in meditating,

and what I had read about life after death, I was not
fearful. Even so, I was a little apprehensive about being
there alone with Paul's body for two hours. As I gazed
at Paul, read, prayed, and sang as the spirit moved me, I
felt close to his spirit and the realm he had crossed into.
This made the time pass quickly and dispelled any fear
and "creepiness" about being around a dead body.

Other friends helped Linda by cleaning her home
and serving donated food to the mourners who kept
streaming in throughout the day and night. They knew
Paul and Linda through work, Waldorf schools, French
connections, and California connections. There were
new friends and old coming and going, gathering in the
house or in the yard. All had access to Paul. Although
most people approached his hut with trepidation, they
found that once they stepped inside and settled in, it
was natural and comforting to have this time to say
goodbye to Paul. When they realized this, parents even
brought their children into the hut for short periods.

Saturday morning, after taking my turn with Paul, I
stayed to clean the kitchen. Paul's relatives came to the
house to be together in their own sorrow and shock. His
parents and sister had said their goodbyes at the hospital. A few of the other relatives slipped out to say goodbye to him in the hut, but most had no interest in being
a part of the vigil or seeing his body. They had their own
time in the living room for memory sharing; then they
were gone.

Sunday afternoon, Dennis, Nina, Soren, and I attended
the last day of the vigil. We were sorry that 14-year old
Kevin was at summer camp and could not join the rest

of our family and friends gathered in the back yard of
the Bergh's home. Three-year-old Soren, who knew Paul
well and had heard us talking about the vigil, wanted to
play his harmonica for Paul. Dennis and I brought him
into the meditation hut at a moment when no one else
was there. We walked up to the coffin with him to look at
Paul. I handed him the harmonica and he fearlessly stood
right there and played an improvised tune while we sat
and watched him give this last gift to Paul.

Nina had stayed with Kirsten other times during this
weekend. She was crucial to Kirsten, for Molly left for
a previously planned wilderness camp in New York the
day after Paul died. Kirsten only gradually became comfortable with going into the hut to be with her father, firt
by bringing a flower, and then going in for a short time
with a friend.

By Sunday evening, Kirsten wanted time with Nina
and some other high school friends alone with Paul.
After a ceremonial send-off with Linda and many other
people crammed into the little house, the girls continued singing to him late into the night. In the end they
finally became comfortable "hanging out with a dead
person," as they called it.

This vigil was a new experience for everyone, a different way of experiencing death. It touched people in deep
ways. It not only dispelled myths and fears, but opened
doors for us to think about our own deaths or that of
others in our families. We learned how to create more
meaningful experiences than modern funeral practices
and traditions dictated. It awakened us to the other side
of life that continues on beyond death. Linda's welcoming

openness to all to be present for Paul wove a fabric of love through our community. Our eyes were opened to the tragedy that could befall any of us, but also to the love that can transcend it.

On Monday morning, after the 72 hours legally allowed for visitation without embalming, the Cremation Society came to take Paul's body to the crematorium. Close friends rode with Linda in a separate car. The crematorium was not set up to accommodate guests, in fact, had never had family members present during a cremation. There were no cushy chairs, pictures on the walls, or music. Linda, Dennis, Patrick, Diana, and other friends stood on a cement floor in a large garage-like room where Paul was put in the retort. They chanted, "The earth, the air, the fire, the water, return, return, return, return," above the roar of the furnace firing up. They stayed until they felt satisfied that they had accompanied Paul as far as they could on his journey here on earth.

That afternoon, we continued the preparation for Paul's memorial service that had been started two days earlier. Linda designed a program, using a drawing Kirsten had done that morning on the cover, and chose songs to sing. Some friends telephoned people; others prepared artistic contributions. I practiced speaking a verse from Corinthians to be done in Eurythmy by Marianne Schneider. Dennis and I rehearsed a piano and saxophone duet.

The next morning Paul's ashes were delivered to Linda. In the flurry of activities, Nina and Kirsten hadn't thought about what they were going to wear to the service. They went through closets in the Bergh and O'Brien households, unable to find anything satisfactory. When a friend who was tall enough offered her closet, both girls found an outfit. Even dressing Nina and Kirsten became a community project!

The memorial service, in the sanctuary of the nearby Lake Harriet Community Church, was a culmination of what had been going on for a week since Paul's hospital admission. There were no clergy involved; Dennis was the emcee of the event, and we created our own ways of remembering Paul. Everyone was given the opportunity to share their memories and thoughts. People came away from the service knowing a little more about Paul Bergh and feeling that our community had been blessed both by his presence and by his passing.

Dennis and I were amazed and grateful that we had heard Paul's life story in March on our trip to Chicago. That was a treasure to last our lifetime, with the story now concluded.

Little did Linda, Dennis, and I know that the next year our shock and grief over losing Paul would be overshadowed by an unimaginable tragedy, and that what we had learned from caring for Paul was preparing us to care for our daughters.

Seventeen

School started again, Nina's junior year. She began to practice for auditions for the fall musical, *Fiddler on the Roof.* She wanted so desperately to continue on this roll of being in plays, of having something in school to look

forward to. She didn't make it into the play. But rather
than withdraw into rejection, Nina applied for the position of student director, which she got. It brought out
a more aggressive, organizational side of Nina which
I hadn't seen before and which was contrary to her
phlegmatic nature. She was a part of the show and thus
the social group, and this was very important. She loved
that show and the whole experience.

Nina celebrated her golden birthday that fall: she
turned 17 on October 17. I remember the beautiful
fall day. Soren and I went walking and gathered golden
leaves to create a collage ironed in wax paper for Nina's
birthday card. Nina was glowing when she came home
from school and play practice, for her friends had all
remembered her birthday very affectionately. She felt
loved. Dennis and I splurged and bought a surprise for
her— a new stereo, for she only had a boom box that
played tapes. Now she could play CDs like everyone else.

The next excitement was Frederique Destailleur's
arrival from France. Fred had planned to come spend a
year with the Bergh family. His father had been Kirsten's
teacher in France the previous year, and Fred and
Kirsten were friends. When Paul died, Fred was not sure
if he should come, but Linda decided to go ahead with
the plan. Perhaps an extra young person around the
house would keep things from getting too sad.

Fred arrived in mid-December. The next day, Linda,
Kirsten, and Fred came to our home for dinner and a
night out to see the "Black Nativity." Fred had an angular
nose and dark hair that fell forward almost into his eyes,
giving him a handsomely disheveled and rugged look.

Nina and Kirsten with Fred at our home

Although Nina was excited to meet Fred, it was slightly awkward because she didn't speak French, and Fred didn't know much English.

After Christmas we all went to the Bergh's cabin for a few days. With Kevin (now 14), Nina, Kirsten, and Fred, there was a lot of youthful energy. The four teenagers went sledding, snowboarding, and frolicking in the snow. In the cozy evenings by the fire, we started off reading *The Hunchback of Notre Dame* out loud together, inspired by Fred's presence and Paul's memory. This was good language practice for Fred, since he was familiar with the story in French. Then the hilarious

pantomimes by Kirsten and Fred began. They had a way
of moving/dancing/lip synching in an improvisatory
duet to the music of *Priscilla: Queen of the Desert* that
had the rest of us in stitches. Both of them were natural
comedians/actors. After Soren and the three adults were
in bed, the teenagers continued late into the night with
music, movies, talking, and laughing in their sleeping
bag island on the living room floor.

On New Year's Eve we had a great bonfire, with
recorded music setting the mood, out on the ice. In the
more somber moments of reflection in our ritual, we
sent our loving thoughts aloft to Paul with the sparks of
the fire. We also felt delirious with the wildness of our
isolation in the north woods, hearing our laughter and
cheers echoing from across the frozen lake.

From that point on, Nina felt a pull to the Bergh
household. With Kirsten, Molly O'Brien, and now Fred
in the same house, it was the place to be, where everything was happening. Many Friday or Saturday nights
we would get a late call saying that she was going to stay
there for the night. Dennis and I were sad that none of
the action was happening at our house, but happy that
Nina had a place where she belonged.

Meanwhile, Nina tried out for the winter play and
again was rejected. She was starting to get discouraged. One Saturday Nina asked me to go with her to a
yarn store to help her buy yarn for a sweater. She chose
a beautiful cardigan pattern in earthy colors. This was
her antidote to depression. Soon after that, school was
called off due to an ice storm and a temperature plunge
to -40 degrees. The power was out for most of the day.

Gwyneth and Nina, spring 1995

Nina, Kevin, Soren, and I huddled by the free-standing gas heater in our added-on family room with the door to the rest of the house closed. While Kevin played solitaire and Soren and I played Go Fish and Old Maid, Nina knit away most of the day.

By spring, Nina had bounced back from her winter depression and was running on high, talking on the phone with Kirsten each day when she came home from school, and frequently getting together with Gwyneth, who was living close by in St. Paul for a short time. She also connected with a group of friends in her orchestra at school during a trip to Colorado. Kevin, who played cello in the Armstrong orchestra, also became a part of this group of friends on this trip. It was a real testament to their close relationship that Nina included him; in fact, he would have been rather lost if it had not been for Nina and her 11th-grade friends reaching out to him.

As the end of the school year approached, many plans for the summer were made. Nina was invited on a camping trip to Itasca State Park in northern Minnesota with a group of girls from school. Later Nina, Kirsten, Molly, Gwyneth, and two other Camphill friends planned to drive in our minivan to a Waldorf youth conference in East Troy, Wisconsin. And finally, the Dietzels and Berghs, along with Molly O'Brien and Fred Destailleur, were planning a backpacking trip to the Bighorn Mountains in Wyoming.

Mountain Magic

Before she went to the youth conference, Nina enjoyed a few weeks of "freedom" just hanging out with her girlfriends. She even drove to a nearby Caribou Coffee by herself once, just to sit and write, and felt very grown up.

Nina's godmother, Laura, now a painter, and the wife of a Waldorf School teacher, came from New York with her two children to visit us and give a painting workshop for teachers and parents at the Waldorf School.

Nina returned from the youth conference while Laura was here. Nina and Kirsten, the youngest participants in the conference, were especially enthusiastic about their experience. They shared with me, Dennis, Laura, and Linda their re-awakened awareness of how different

Waldorf high school education was from what they were getting in public school. The workshops in astronomy, painting, singing, and biodynamic gardening, as well as new friendships with Waldorf school graduates, fed their souls. They didn't want to go back to their regular schools. They needed to find a Waldorf school where they could finish high school.

Dennis and I already were in the midst of meetings with a group of students and parents who wanted to start a Waldorf high school in Minneapolis. It would begin with ninth and tenth grades and thus would not include Nina or Kirsten, but was a possibility for Kevin. He discussed with Laura and us his conflicting feelings. His experience at public school in 9th grade was a mix of excitement at the opportunities opening up for him in acting and writing, and feeling like a loner as he trudged from class to class amidst the throngs of students. The 10th grade students who were initiating the push for a Waldorf high school pursued Kevin, for there was only one other boy involved. He decided to become a part of this pioneering Waldorf class.

"What about me?" came Nina's undemanding voice after waiting through deliberations with Kevin. We then turned to the possibilities for her. One was Hawthorne Valley School, a K–12 Waldorf school in Harlemville, New York where Laura's husband taught. Nina and Kirsten checked out schools in California and Pennsylvania. They decided that, with the connection to Laura, Hawthorne Valley looked most promising. Laura would go back to New York and investigate housing possibilities. Nina and Kirsten got applications. After having one

Nina and Kevin, summer 1996

year free of tuition payments, Dennis and I were reeling at the serious financial commitment we were getting into with two teenagers in private schools.

Nina again accompanied Kirsten to her cabin, along with Molly, Fred, and one other boy, for Kirsten's 17th birthday celebration. It was only when she came back, and was really down in the dumps, that I became aware that Nina had been in love with Fred for a long time. The weekend up north had been miserable, as it seemed a relationship between Fred and Molly was blooming, and Nina felt helplessly betrayed after having had a romance of sorts with him. She had withdrawn from most of the group interactions, able to express herself only to

Kirsten. Nina did not share this with me in a mother-daughter heart to heart. It was through Linda that I got the information. I was sad that I was not able to take her in my arms and comfort her, but could only acknowledge what she was going through indirectly.

Here we were, ALL (including Fred and Molly) soon to go on a backpacking trip together for two weeks. How was this going to play itself out?

In the car on the first day of our trip, Nina and Kirsten finished their applications for Hawthorne Valley School, including a sketch of a human being which Nina agonized over. We mailed them in Fargo, North Dakota. We drove a long way that day, switching drivers and car occupants frequently. Riding in Linda's van was most popular due to the CD player. We became familiar with some of the teenagers' favorite music just by hearing snatches when we came to a rest stop. We were drawn to the African music from the soundtrack of "The Power of One" that we heard frequently.

Dennis and I could see for ourselves that Fred and Molly were getting close. In the next three nights of camping along the way, the young people seemed to be figuring out how to relate together as a group in an amiable way. Kevin was new to the configuration. His companionship with Fred probably provided a good diffusion of the intensity of the romantic tangle.

When we finally reached the mountains, we could feel the geographic and mental shift; we all could begin to exhale. We woke early on the day of the start of our wilderness adventure to pack up our backpacks and meet our guide, who provided horses for carrying our food

Kirsten, Molly, and Nina on their overnight adventure

and for Soren (four years old) and Linda to ride on. The rest of us donned our backpacks. Only Kevin and Fred found this to be completely enjoyable as they strode out with bounce in their step, always far ahead of us. The rest of us remembered what a challenge backpacking was, even though we had worked on getting in shape.

Despite aching muscles, our seven days in the wilderness were glorious. We thrived on granola, prunes,

Molly, Nina, and Kirsten back from their overnight

Wasa rye crackers, hummus, and the occasional fresh lake trout. Our days were free to wander to mountain streams, slopes of boulders, or meadows of wild flowers, to sit and watch the pica family living under the rocks, or to read or write in solitude. Fred, Dennis, and Kevin took a few day trips on which they could tire themselves out to their hearts' content. Molly, Kirsten, and Nina went on their own trek up a mountain, lugging all their equipment for an overnight in their backpacks, determined not to be outdone by the men. We were relieved when they returned safely. They were triumphant in their accomplishment. Linda and I were content to bask in our free time and have mini-adventures closer to the campsite with Soren.

There was also plenty of time for "hanging out." A few times we sensed that something intense was going on in the tent where the teenagers were talking. But they had a way of working things out. They remained close and companionable, all very physical in their affection for each other. We marveled at the depth and intensity of their commitments to their relationships. A myriad of feelings were expressed in various creative outpourings inspired by our idyllic surroundings. Molly shared a poem with us around the campfire one evening after the girls' overnight.

THEM

by Molly O'Brien   July 19, 1995

They flow together
Like a pair of shoes.
Molded out of laughter
They make their treads,
As girls gentle and silly,
As women wise and compassionate,
Light and dark in both.
Sunburnt and beautiful,
As maidens they bathe.
The mountain stream gently caresses them.
Blowing in the wind as prairie grass
They bend but do not break,
For strength and love are their souls.
Echoing along the creases of their smiles
Are dreams of mountain houses and gurgling streams.
Wrapped in these lovely's arms
No pain is unbearable and hope is always present.

This poem expressed the magic that was being woven in the mountains. At the time, it was interesting to us that Molly wrote about Nina and Kirsten as a pair. She was looking at them from a step back, coupled as she was now with Fred, but still friends with them. After Nina and Kirsten were gone, it seemed uncanny that the one left behind had written about the two who had strode away together, away from her. It was as if the stage was being set for the great drama that would be enacted, the actors already taking on their roles.

We packed up our camp once and moved on to the campsite where our guide would meet us on the last day. Without a horse on this part of the trip, Soren tried to hike, but ended up being carried in turn by Fred, Kevin, and Dennis, along with their own backpacks. He was just too little to keep up. He enjoyed the attention. When we stopped to rest in the shade, Soren was in the middle of the heap of bodies, friendly with everyone.

One morning Dennis and I sat with Kirsten and Nina in the sun on the steep slope overlooking the second campsite, and discussed the Hawthorne Valley School in New York. We had concerns about the two girls rooming together. Would this be the best situation for each of them to find their way in a new social milieu? Would Nina have sufficient space to take initiative at her own pace, or would she just coast along in Kirsten's shadow? They assured us that they recognized their differences, and that their tight bond could be excluding to others, but they were determined to support each other in making their own way. After all, they wouldn't be in the same class, so when would they see each other if they didn't live together? They wanted to experience this adventure together. Eventually Dennis and I had to trust their judgment.

Goodbyes

After we got home from Wyoming, phone interviews with Hawthorne Valley faculty confirmed Nina and Kirsten's acceptance into the 12th and 11th grades, respectively. There were now three and a half weeks left of life as we knew it, with our three children under one roof. Suddenly we were caught up in a whirlwind of preparations for a new life and farewells to the old. Nina had to face all of her high school friends whom she was leaving behind. She had to see Fred off to France and bid adieu to her first, tumultuous, and in the end, unrequited, love. And she had to part with Gwyneth and Annamaria once again, the three of them moving to far-flung places to meet their destinies.

Nina's closest friend at Armstrong, Bethany Thorsen, lived right around the corner from our house. She had met Nina at the bus stop the first day Nina went to Armstrong in the 10th grade. Bethany was at least 6 inches shorter than Nina, but much more outgoing and talkative. By spring of sophomore year, Bethany was picking Nina up every morning in the Mercury Sable her parents gave her when she turned 16, eating her Twix Bar and drinking Jolt for breakfast as she drove. They were a most unlikely pair, but loved each other dearly. Bethany was out of town most of the summer. When Nina told her the news of her going to school in New York State, Bethany wrote back:

I fear coming home for many reasons. One being I have changed and grown so much up here that I fear I will no longer fit at home. Another is that I don't know if I want to fit. Home seems so distant and story-like. I also don't want to come home to say goodbye to you. I know that we will never not be kindred spirits, and that thought comforts me more than you know. But, parting with you will be difficult and painful. I need you to follow your heart so that I have the strength to follow mine.

Another high school classmate, Alexis, wrote a note that echoed the sentiments of several others:

I am so glad that I have gotten to know you over the past year. Your friendship has truly been a blessing to me. I wish you all the joy in the world. I know that this is not goodbye forever, but I just want you to know that you are a very special person.

I feel as if I've known you forever and yet we have only gotten to know each other in the past year. I know that I've told you this before but I really do feel this closeness to you that I really can't explain.

Anyway, enough of this mushy stuff; the point is you're a great friend and a great person and I'll miss you. I wish you endless happiness always. I love you for being you!

Two nights before Nina left for New York I sat in the living room talking with her about living on her own,

managing her finances, finding a job, and applying for
college even though she was thinking about a year off
before she went. I also felt impelled to encourage her
one more time to find a balance between exercise and
diet to manage her weight more effectively. It was a last
attempt at exerting my motherly influence out of love
and concern for her well being, unpleasant as that part
of the conversation was for both of us.

The evening before Nina left, our family planned a
dinner out to Nina's favorite vegetarian restaurant. In
the afternoon, I went on a housekeeping frenzy. I doled
out jobs to each family member and took to the vacuum
cleaner myself, defying any dust to defile a single corner
in my house. I was unstoppable, out of control. All the
while, I chastised myself inwardly, asking, "Is this the
way you want Nina to remember her last day at home?"

After an hour and a half, however, the frenzy was
over. I was able to relax and savor the festive and poignant mood of that last meal we would have together
as a family of five. We don't go out to eat often, and
choosing a classy Minneapolis restaurant made it feel
like the extra special occasion it was. With two ragtag
teenagers, whose best shoes were either Birkenstock
sandals (Nina), or sneakers (Kevin), and a sweet-natured
and adorable blond 4-year-old boy, we were not the
typical party dining in the high-ceilinged Café Brenda.
Nina was affectionate with Soren, as always, enjoying
snuggling with him on her lap, or taking him for a walk,
when a diversion was needed. She chatted amiably with
Kevin about shared summer memories and his future at
the new Waldorf "Youth Initiative." We all talked about

writing letters and future holidays together and the fabulous food we were eating, fresh walleye or rainbow trout with unusual sauces or relishes for some, soba noodle salad or buckwheat croquettes for others.

Later that evening, after Soren was in bed, Nina did last minute packing in her bedroom off the living room with some friends. I sat in the living room writing a farewell card to Nina. In the quiet of the summer evening, I had a vision of my dear girl, now an individual in her own right. I saw her strengths and weaknesses, now not as a mother in the earthly sense wanting to have some influence, but as a mother in the cosmic sense.

As the subdued voices of Nina and her friends reached me from the bedroom, I sensed how Dennis and I had provided the ancestral stream she chose to unite with, the physical vessel for this incarnation. She came to earth on a path she chose, to provide the learning conditions for her karmic unfolding. And I saw that the name we had given her held the secrets of her being (from the character of each letter as expressed in the art of Eurythmy).

I shared my vision of Nina and the lines I had written with Dennis, and together we wrote an inscription on cardstock cut from a pastel watercolor-wash painting:

"As you embark on your journey, we affirm your being as an individual with these thoughts on your name. Within it are four sounds which express polarities which are the challenges and gifts of your life. You are the balancing point between these polarities. May your journey be blessed!"

N   I struggle to bring to light parts of my inner being
I   I feel the strength of my eternal Self forging into the
  future
N   I shy away from meeting the world
A   Yet I am open to all the wonders streaming to me
  from above, below, behind and before.

Looking back on that day, I think I needed that housekeeping frenzy to create some order in a life that felt as if it were falling apart. Saying farewell to my 17-year-old daughter had come too fast. I needed to feel more in control. I also needed to clear the space to make an opening to receive inspiration.

Nina read the card without any outward reaction before she opened her gift at the airport the next day. She expressed a sincere thank you, but without a profusion of words or hugs. I don't really know how she received it or what it meant to her. However, I like to think that it was a blessing to her, giving her the freedom to meet her destiny. Little could I imagine at the time what that destiny would be. This vision of Nina's higher being, I am sure, was part of my preparation for accepting it.

Kirsten and Nina at the airport, August 31, 1996

Fulfillment

Eighteen

On the morning of August 31, 1996, our family accompanied Nina to the airport, meeting Linda and Kirsten at the departure gate. The two girls were exuberant, for they had gone through the sad farewells and were excited that their new life was about to begin.

The enormity of their departure did not hit me until we got home. I went into Nina's room and discovered that she had efficiently packed away almost every trace of herself. The beloved picture of the little girl by the birch tree with fairies in its branches that Annamaria had painted for her was in the closet! The postcard collection lining her windows was gone! The dried roses hanging from the curtain rod were in the trash can! I suddenly realized that Nina was really gone. I cried and cried as I laid on her futon bed without the familiar maroon down comforter, watched by the fairies in the flowing new-leafed tree Kirsten had painted on her wall. This sweet, sunny room, the best bedroom in the house, would feel empty and lonely without its caretaker. Still sobbing, I retrieved the dried roses from the garbage, and repositioned Annamaria's painting on Nina's bookshelf, not ready to erase her presence from the room.

A beautiful fall followed. As the leaves on our maple trees turned crimson and gold, and then drifted to the ground, Dennis and I mourned the passing of a stage of life that Nina's leaving marked. It was an unspoken leitmotif between us, acknowledged with occasional sighs and leaning into one another. Only I, at odd moments, especially on the weekends when our family was home together without Nina, would break into tears. Kevin and Soren cowered in the background, not knowing how to behave when someone had such outbursts of feeling. My firstborn leaving home had come too suddenly. I had thought I had her senior year to prepare for it, but instead Nina was over a thousand miles away for the 12th grade.

We phoned Nina every couple of weeks, but mostly corresponded through the mail. It was comforting for me to share some of the details of our life with Nina in letters.

Nina had always written very satisfying letters to us when she was away from home. Every time she went to camp, she had a period of homesickness, when she would express appreciation for the home she loved so dearly.

This time she didn't go through the homesick stage. She wrote, "I am still waiting for homesickness to set in (no, I'm not waiting, it's just not coming!) This all just seems so very normal and just how it should be." Later Nina wrote, "With Kirsten here all is bearable. No matter what happens we are quite happy with ourselves." Her letters showed more objectivity and maturity in dealing with all that came her way. The whole family loved reading them.

One late September afternoon as I was making supper, Nina called out of the blue.

"You know those sunflower-carrot patties you make? Can you give me the recipe?"

Nina and Kirsten were living with Bruce and Karen Frishkoff, a high school teacher and his wife. They shared household responsibilities, and tonight was Nina's turn to cook.

"I just wanted to pretend that you lived down the street, Mama, and I could just call you for a recipe."

Nina was slowly making a place for herself in her senior class at Hawthorne Valley School.

My afternoon artistic class is stained glass. So glad I am about that. A very dear teacher and we have six weeks just to design and make our own piece. Then we have stone sculpting. Wow! (September 5)

Each day I return to school is better than the last. Kirsten and I were talking today about how lovely it is to be able to look forward to going back to school after the weekend. . . . Perhaps it is ideal to be away from Waldorf and then return so as to be able to see the beauty. (September 15)

Bruce and Karen Frishkoff lived at the top of a long hill that led down to the hamlet of Harlemville. Hawthorne Valley School, with the related biodynamic farm and farm store right across the street, was the center of the town. Nina and Kirsten walked down Fern Hill's steep gravel road every morning to get to school, passing a dozen or so other houses belonging to teachers or other families. After school, Nina had two jobs on alternating days. She worked on the grounds crew at the school, and she prepared supper for an elderly couple who lived next to the school. When the jobs were done, she hiked back up the hill to go home. "Endless hiking!" she exclaimed in another letter.

Nina was thinking about college. She had narrowed her interests to a few schools and wanted to visit one. I was invited to make this trip with her, a great excuse for me to visit her November 6–11, 1996.

Meanwhile, Nina's birthday, October 17, was approaching. Before Nina left for New York, she had purchased fabric to sew a white tiered skirt like one that a friend of hers had. She had cut it out, but had gotten no further. Now I took on the project of completing the skirt for her birthday. With Soren by my side, I chose lace to go in-between the tiers and sewed the skirt and an underskirt. I sent this gift along with Molly when she flew out to visit the girls on Nina's birthday weekend. This was the first time one of our children had celebrated a birthday away from home. The skirt was a way of making our love a tangible part of Nina's celebration.

Nina, however, was sick that weekend. She couldn't do anything but lay in bed. This did not deter her new group of friends from coming over on Saturday night for what was supposed to have been a birthday party. They went up to Nina's room where they pampered her with a foot massage and serenaded her with guitar and singing.

Later that month I got another afternoon call. Nina was in tears over her senior practicum. Nina's senior project was to write and produce a play. For her practicum, she had arranged to "shadow" a woman who ran a theater in Hudson, New York. When the time came for the practicum, however, the woman was out of town.

Nina was not a girl who cried often. She was even-keeled and not given to drama; I was taken aback by her sobbing and felt helpless. There was nothing I could do but be sympathetic. I encouraged her to talk to someone there who could help her figure out an alternative. Later that week, she wrote that she had gone to Laura, who "was an angel. It made all of the difference in the world to talk to her. She's so open-minded and optimistic. This week I am going to work with Laura on color and maybe some others on music and movement so that I can come to my play through these different mediums."

The letter ended, "I can't wait 'til you come, Mama!"

A Visit

On Wednesday, November 6, I flew to Albany, New York, and rented a car to drive one hour south to Harlemville. I turned off the Taconic Parkway onto the road that leads two miles to the town. As I approached the school, I saw two girls walking arm in arm. One was Nina. I got out and waved, and they came running to me. Nina looked different. She had on clothes I didn't recognize. She was not with Kirsten, but with someone I'd never seen. Rachel, whom Nina had told me about, happened to be the daughter of an old friend of mine. We had known each other twenty years before, and had shared birth announcements of our first babies, Rachel

"The Angels of Harlemville"

Marie Wetmore and Nina Christine Dietzel. Although I hadn't kept up the correspondence with Rachel's mother, here they were, the two baby girls who had never met, arm in arm.

The sight of Nina with this new friend and new (though, per her choice, old and shabby second hand) clothes gave a jolt to my heart. It was a combination of joy that Nina was so obviously in love with her new life, and sadness that she had grown away from me. She would buy clothes on her own and do many other things that I wouldn't be a part of.

Nina and I left Rachel and drove up Fern Hill to the Frishkoffs' house. Kirsten was there, for now she was sick and had stayed home from school. We three sat in Nina's room looking at everything they wanted to show me. In Nina's window hung an 18 x 15-inch, oval, stained glass piece. I was awestruck. It was a freeform design with a two-pronged flame in the lower middle and a rainbow of colors raying out from it. Nina told me all about making it. She showed me one painting that she had done with Laura. It was also so delicately beautiful that I was overwhelmed by the artistry that had blossomed here. She said she wanted to send the painting home with me, but I thought she might need something to show for her senior practicum at the end of the year, and should keep it there.

Then they showed me Nina's bedside table. Kirsten had made it for her in her joinery class! It was an unusual form, an irregular half moon set on three legs. It was totally charming sitting there with Nina's candle, incense, and book on it.

The girls sat on either side of me on Nina's single bed, showing me the pictures of their classmates. They told me what they knew about each person and the special qualities of their relationship to him or her. I guess this was my orientation. The next day I would be visiting school and seeing these people, so I needed to know about them.

On Thursday morning, I sat in on Nina's chemistry main lesson block (a subject studied in depth for several weeks in a double period every morning). The lesson started with a verse, then poetry recitation and a song, the way morning lessons are started in every grade in a Waldorf School. These students, some who had been doing this for 12 years, still could enter into this with some reverence. The chemistry lesson was totally engaging due to the great enthusiasm and practical approach of the teacher. I felt so grateful for this enlightened education Nina was receiving.

I had lunch with Laura at the Summer's self-designed country home/painting studio over the hill behind the school, getting her impression of the girls' Harlemville experience. Nina and Kirsten came to her house every Saturday morning for pancakes, so she remained in close touch with them. Her familiarity with the people and situations surrounding them gave me another view of their life in this small community.

After school, I picked the girls up, and we were off to Long Island University. I drove while the girls snacked on the wheat-free spice cake that Laura had made for them, breaking off chunks with their fingers. Then Nina took over and drove for three or four hours into the dark, around New York City. I was impressed by her stamina.

Finally, we stopped for supper at a chain restaurant. Kirsten engaged the waitress, Darlene, in conversation while Nina and I looked at the menu. Both Nina and Kirsten were vegetarians, and I was almost a vegetarian, so we ordered the stir-fry. Kirsten, without even looking at the menu, said she'd have the same thing. When it came, she found that it included the one vegetable she did not like. Kirsten picked out all of the broccoli, and never let on to Darlene that the stir-fry was less than perfect. As we left the restaurant, she called, "Have a nice night, Darlene!"

Kirsten clearly took the lead in this situation, her outgoing nature bubbling forth in the pauses of our more thoughtful natures. She reminded me so much of her father, Paul.

Late Thursday night we arrived at our motel in Southampton. Our appointments at the Friends' World Program were on Friday morning. Friends' World occupies a small corner of Long Island University. Many of the classes are held in dormitory basement rooms furnished with well-used couches and chairs. It is a small program and its 100 students are required to be on campus only for their first semester. After that, they are working "in the field" in the United States or at one of seven campuses worldwide. Students design their own programs or choose from several model programs. They do their work/study in at least two foreign countries over their four years.

The visit confirmed Nina's attraction to this unique approach to a college education. It was very informal, intimate and friendly, and the students we saw were clearly non-conformists. This appealed to Nina, who was not interested in the traditional route to a traditional career. She had nascent interests in herbs and healing, and always wanted to travel. She hadn't been able to imagine where she would fit in, but here was a place! One of the model programs was in healing and holistic therapies, with India being one of the countries to study in. She had always longed to go to India. This was perfect!

Kirsten and Nina, November 8, 1996

Kirsten, though a year younger, was interested in this program, also. She accompanied Nina to her interview (with Nina's consent) with a reminder from me that it was Nina's interview, not hers. After the interview, we spent several hours walking along the beach, playing with the waves, collecting rocks and other ocean treasures. I was happily filling my pockets with shells and polished stones. Kirsten was finding gifts for her friend Zusha's family. Nina was content to just look and admire or give intriguing objects to me. I took some pictures of Nina and Kirsten as the sun set over the ocean.

When we got back to the motel, I changed my clothes

and got my hairbrush to put myself back together after being buffeted by the salty ocean wind. Kirsten observed that Nina was just like me; she was changing her clothes and brushing her hair, too. I could see that Nina and I liked to keep ourselves well put together and not get too far "out there," whereas Kirsten was not bothered by hair out of place or damp, salty pants; she could just plunge into the next thing "as is." I was pleased by Kirsten's observation; I hadn't noticed that Nina had taken on any of my characteristics.

That night we went out for supper and then to see the movie, Romeo and Juliet. On Saturday we took a leisurely drive home, opting for the scenic route. We stopped at tag sales and antique stores as our whim dictated. When I used a phone at a gas station to call home, we noticed a Dunkin' Donuts shop next door and Nina wanted to get some donuts. We entered the store, giddy with the excitement of rows of raised, cake and filled doughnuts, crullers, long johns, and Danish. Nina and Kirsten went for the chocolate glazed, while I settled on the custard filled. We giggled as we sat and took bites from our melt-in-the mouth fried delights, an unheard of frivolity in our family. I was in the mood to be carefree, for a trip without a four-year-old was a rare treat.

When we got back to Harlemville, we visited the Elinson family. Zusha Elinson, a boy in Kirsten's 11th grade class, with an unusual head of frizzy black hair to match his unusual name, had become a close friend. He and his friend Seamus had a band that practiced at the Elinson's country home. These practices often became social events that Nina and Kirsten attended. Through this, the girls, especially Kirsten, became close to Zusha's parents, Cecelia and Bob Elinson, and his younger sister Sarah. That night Kirsten gave her gifts to each of them. While Nina and Kirsten hung out with the kids, I sat in the kitchen visiting with Cecelia, a beloved projects teacher at Hawthorne Valley lower school, and Bob, a car mechanics teacher at a vocational school in Hudson, whose eyes sparkled with an impish sense of humor. The Elinsons, a very warm family, attracted many people to their circle.

I was especially curious to meet Sarah, age 14, as Nina told me that when Sarah saw a picture of Kevin with long, wavy hair that I had sent on Nina's birthday, she immediately fell in love with him. Sarah had the same dark eyes as her brother, but her auburn hair was straight and long, and she had an outgoing and solicitous way of relating to people.

Kirsten schemed to keep this group of friends together into the future. Now that Kevin was in the picture with Sarah, it was perfect. Kirsten and Zusha, Nina and Seamus, and Kevin and Sarah—each had a match which would result in marriage, and then they would all be related! It was quite amusing.

On Sunday we planned to visit with my brother, Alan, who lived in Vermont. He was driving down (without his family) and would arrive at the Frishkoff's that morning. At the appointed time, Nina, Kirsten, and I walked down Fern Hill to meet him. Kirsten was eager to meet Nina's beloved uncle. Alan stopped his car when he saw us and got out to hug us. I had put a new roll of film in the camera and took a shot of him with Nina and Kirsten, the last picture I was to take on this visit.

Alan Mitter-Burke, Nina, and Kirsten on Fern Hill,
November 10, 1996

It was a beautiful fall day, and we took a cross-country hike from the Frishkoff home through the woods
to a cafe on the next road over. Nina and Kirsten hiked
together, and Alan and I had time to visit. We talked
about our mother's degenerating health and our stepfather, Wayne. My mom had visited Minnesota in August,
so I was acquainted with her condition. Her Parkinson's
disease was becoming harder to manage.

Hallucinations at night were difficult for Wayne to
cope with. Dealing with infirm elderly parents was a
new challenge, and particularly difficult since Alan and I
lived so far away from them.

The four of us had a delightful lunch together at the cafe, and then walked back to the Frishkoff's on a country road. This time we all walked together and kept up a lively conversation, full of laughter.

That evening, after another visit with Laura, my visit to Harlemville was almost over. I longed for a last bit of intimacy with Nina, but didn't know how to connect with her. She was so tight with Kirsten that she didn't need anything more from me. Though I was reluctant to leave, I knew it was time. Would our mother-daughter relationship be like mine with my mother? When we visited it was good for a while, then became old, and time for my mother and me to go back to our separate lives. It made me sad to think that my relationship with Nina might be no different.

Because the girls had Monday, November 11, off from school, I didn't want to wake them early to see me off, but I crept in to Nina's bedroom for one last glimpse of my beautiful daughter sleeping. I would like to say that I took her in my arms and told her how beautiful she was and that I loved her. However, this was not in my repertoire. I was not embraced and kissed by my mother. I felt loved by her, but also criticized often. When I looked at Nina sleeping, I held these same conflicting emotions. I was filled with love and the anticipation of missing her when I returned home, but also with unmet expectations. I had hoped somehow to find her changed. I had fantasized about finding her 20 pounds thinner, shedding the weight that had gradually accumulated over her teenage years, in the two months of being on her own in Harlemville.

I was afraid that her appearance would get in the way of her being loved by a nice young man.

All I could manage in that moment was a light hug and a kiss on Nina's cheek with the words, "Last kiss until Christmastime!"

I walked out of the bedroom with tears on my cheeks, got in the car, and drove to the airport. I left Nina and Kirsten asleep on Fern Hill.

As I reflected later on these last moments with Nina, I rationalized that these were the normal thoughts of concern of a parent for her child. I tucked away that part of my memory, unwilling to listen to the stream trickling deep under the ice and snow of my frozen heart.

Life in Harlemville

November 19, '96
Dear Dad, Mom, Kevin, and Soren,
I got your letter and pictures today and I realized it had been a long time since I'd written. These days it seems as though I could sit around and write letters to no end and still have more to write. It is a grey cold day outside—we woke to rain pattering on the roof and it soon turned to wet snow. No snow on the ground yet though! We had an amazingly warm sunny day on Sunday, sort of like early October weather in MN. We cut, stacked and hauled wood in the sunshine.

We had a rather dull weekend. On Friday there was a dance at school with Rhythm in Smoke playing (Zusha and Seamus' band). It was really dumb 'cause no one danced except us. On Saturday we went to the library and to Summer's for pancakes. Sasha slept over. Next weekend promises to be much better. On Friday afternoon I am driving down to Kimberton for the Senior conference. As it turns out only about ten of us from my class are going because it was an option. I'll be saying with Lia. I'm so so excited to see her! Ben ('member the one you labeled as the "all American nice boy" Mom?) has a flying license and a plane—he might fly a couple of us down! Good gosh life is exciting, isn't it?

Our class is still all tied up about the Bahamas. It's strange, though I am new, I have gotten very caught up in everything—Rachel chose me as the only one in the class who would understand her to confide her true feelings about the trip in. Others also chose me to complain to about her. It is all so complex and silly at the same time. At first I was kind of neutral about the whole thing, but now I have become rather partial to the idea of the Bahamas. As my life seems to be going so far, I doubt that I would go there or any place like it on my own, so it's a nice opportunity. The other day I made massive amounts of veggie chowder to sell at school as part of our class trip fundraiser.

Yesterday was Karen's birthday. I made her dinner and a divine chocolate cake and Kirsten made her a card and we sang and lit candles and all. She was very touched because they haven't had a birthday celebration for many years for whatever reason. I like to think how nice it must be for Karen and Bruce to have us here adding a little life to the household (or a lot as the case happens to be!) since it has been quiet for so many years since their boys left.

Thanks so much for the program and photos! It made me rather nostalgic for Armstrong and that whole crew.

Have a lovely feast on Thanksgiving if I don't talk to you before that.

Much love, Nina

Thanksgiving Day

Nina called us on Sunday evening, November 24, when she returned from the senior's conference. She hadn't flown there after all; she had driven with another friend. She was "full" of her experience at the Kimberton Waldorf School in Kimberton, Pennsylvania: Staying at Lia's house (Lia's family lived at Camphill Kimberton) with two other girls from Chicago, talking late into the night, singing at the conference, and meeting up with an old friend from the Minnesota Waldorf School who now went to the Kimberton High School. Lia's family invited Nina to come back down to Kimberton for Thanksgiving with them. Nina was sounding us out about this. If the train was cheap, would it be a good idea? Should she rather stay in Harlemville for Linda's visit? Was it too much to try to fit that in before the trip to Vermont with Linda and Kirsten on Monday? We just encouraged her to check on train fares and make a decision from there.

We had a long conversation and at the end there was a pause, a silence waiting for something beyond comfortable chatter to fill it. Uncomfortably, I said something like it was time to say goodbye for now, and Nina ended with "Give my love to the Potters!" (They were our friends from Camphill who were coming to our house for Thanksgiving.)

On Thursday, Thanksgiving Day, I picked up Linda at 8:30 AM to take her to the airport to fly to Harlemville. I asked Linda if she had heard whether Nina was going to be around for the weekend or not. Linda had not heard, so I said, "I'll have to call her when I get home to find out."

When I got home, Thanksgiving preparations were well underway. I was trying out new vegetable side dishes to accompany the turkey, so I got right to them. Nancy and Steve Potter and their two children arrived on the early side of punctual, true to form. They brought along Kevin's friends from Camphill, Nic and Ciaran, and the pumpkin pies. I served the hors d'oeuvres, a divine Brie baked with cranberry sauce and kiwi, served with crackers. In due time, we gathered for dinner. The squash stuffed with wild rice and apricots, yams with ginger and pear, and garlicky green beans were a huge success and a good feast was had by all. With washing up and the proverbial walk after dinner, the day passed and the Potter family left.

I never called Nina!

Thoughts of Nina

The next morning at breakfast, Kevin, Nic, and Ciaran were thinking about their day. Nic had a record player he needed to have repaired at a special shop in Dinkytown (a neighborhood near the University of Minnesota). Then they wanted to go Christmas shopping in Uptown. Kevin's big question was, "What would be a good present for Nina?" He later told me that while taking the dog for a walk after breakfast, he entertained that question for the entire walk.

Before everyone was ready to leave, Soren and I, looking through a box of cards, found a pouch made by Nina when she was very small, which I had filled with precious little books and valentines and birthday cards she had made. We looked at every one of them, thinking of our sweet girl. Then Soren sat down and "wrote" (in scribbles) a letter to Nina and had me write on it, "Soren and Nina." We left it lying on the coffee table in the living room.

PART II

November 29, 1996

✳

The Day after Thanksgiving in Golden Valley

Dennis went to work as usual on this Friday morning. At 12:20 he received a telephone call. Laura Summer, calling from Harlemville, New York, requested that he be in a private room. Laura minced no words. Nina was dead.

She told him the details. Dennis informed his employer. Then he drove home—how, he doesn't know. He was numb, as if in a trance.

When he arrived at the empty house, he saw on the coffee table Soren's letter to Nina.

He made phone calls to close friends Victor Toso, Kim Pilgrim, and David Leighton. Then he wrapped a shawl around his shoulders and lay on the couch in agonizing solitude, waiting for us to arrive home.

Half an hour later, Dennis heard the garage door open. He walked downstairs and told me to come upstairs. He brought Soren and me to the couch in our family room. He minced no words either. There had been a car accident. Nina and Kirsten had been killed instantly. Linda was in critical condition.

Why Linda? That was my first thought. Why would she still be alive? She was not the one who needed to live. Why would she be left with no husband and no daughter?

Then I closed my eyes and pictured my daughter ascending into the heavens. Nina, Nina, Nina, you are so beautiful. This is all I could think. Dennis tells me I cried, but I didn't think I did. I might have moaned out a question or two to get a picture of what had really happened. The details were superfluous to the fact that Nina was dead. I wanted only to be there with her, wherever she was. How could this have happened while we were carrying on our mundane lives?

When my tears came, I wrapped myself in Dennis's arms and reached out to include Soren. He was not crying, and he did not want to cuddle with us. He was getting paper and crayons. Then he stood by the piano bench drawing pictures. He told us about each one, relating the images to things of the physical world, like fireplaces and smoke. But what we saw in one was a picture of a little human figure and a huge bubble surrounding it. It was as if he wanted to show us through his pictures where Nina was, for he seemed to have a more direct perception of the expansion of her soul. One of the pictures he cut into pieces for a puzzle.

The phone rang. It was David Leighton calling us to lend moral support. I asked him if I needed to start calling people, and he answered that I only should do what I needed for myself.

I was getting the chills. I was probably in shock. I took some arnica tablets and wrapped myself in a blanket.

Soon I wanted my friends to come and be with me. I knew that I needed all the help I could get. I called Barbara, who lived the closest to us, who said she would walk right down. Then I thought of Bethany, Nina's dear friend from high school who lived just around the corner. How could I tell her such a terrible thing? I must, and I did, inviting her to come over, too.

Victor Toso called to confer with us about flights to New York. No, we could not leave that afternoon. We would have to wait until the next morning.

Suddenly I remembered Kevin, wandering around Uptown, not knowing that his sister had died. I was frantic. We had to find Kevin and get him home. We called Tim Pilgrim and asked him to drive around Uptown, find Kevin, Nic, and Ciaran, and bring them home. Tim did that while Kim Pilgrim came over with 3-year-old Rachael and baby Noah.

People started to arrive. It was already twilight. We lit candles. When Barbara's husband Michael came, he and Barbara made soup from our leftover turkey. We sat around the table eating food for comfort. I got out the pictures I had taken on that last visit with Nina, a mere three weeks ago, which now looked so precious and unbelievable. I looked at them with Bethany and her dad, and asked her if she would get copies made for us, and perhaps an enlargement? I didn't even know Bethany's dad, but I didn't at all mind having him there; I was glad to know he was with Bethany, supporting her in going through the death of her friend.

Miracle of miracles, Tim Pilgrim arrived. He had found the three boys at Border's bookstore, the first

place he looked in Uptown. He only told them that
I wanted them home right away. We took them into
Nina's bedroom and told them the news. They didn't
cry. Ciaran and Kevin showed us the Christmas presents
they had each just bought for Nina. Ciaran had bought
a pair of candles, and Kevin had bought a candle in the
shape of a whale. It was heart-wrenching.

At one point, as the evening went on, I laid my head
down in my arms on the table with Bethany's dad sitting
across from me. It felt odd to be showing my helpless-
ness in front of an almost stranger, but I didn't care. I
knew that just by being a father of a girl Nina's age, he
would understand. Somehow, having someone there
who was not a close friend, but could share my sorrow,
cut through the normal boundaries of propriety and
created intimacy.

At some point, everyone left our house, and then
we felt the emptiness in our family. Calls kept coming,
each one harder than the last. Up to 11:00 PM, we were
still hearing from friends who wanted to reach out to us
when they heard the news. Dennis called his parents,
and then my mother and brothers, who were visiting
together in Bloomington, Indiana. That was a call I
didn't care to make. It was hard enough for me to imagine where they were sitting and how they would react to
those unexpected words piercing their ordered lives.

Dennis and I both got on the phone to call Patrick and Diana O'Brien, the Bergh's housemates. The
O'Brien's were directly affected by the accident on three
accounts: the death of Kirsten, who was like a daughter
and sister, the serious injury to Linda, who was like a

sister and mother, and the death of Nina, who was their close friend. Diana immediately began to wail inconsolably, so we could only talk to Patrick. Their holiday reverie at their cabin on the shore of Lake Superior was suddenly filled with tragedy.

After Soren was in bed, I started packing clothes into a suitcase. We all had some decent clothes that weren't in the wash. Even though getting a suitcase packed in time for a departure is a recurrent bad dream for me, I managed to do it efficiently, assisted, I am sure, by a higher power than my own anxious self. Incredibly tired in body and soul, getting ready for bed, meeting by the towel rack in the bathroom, Dennis took me in his arms and said, "I am going to miss her so much!" I could not even fathom missing her; it was too tame of a word for what I was feeling. I couldn't look ahead to what life might look like in the future. I didn't want to go there. Although we cried in each other's arms, my husband and I could not comfort each other. The same pain for which there was no comfort gripped us both.

The Accident

It took us several weeks to piece together the story of how the accident happened, perhaps because we weren't able to take in the details. On that first day, all we knew was that Kirsten was driving. Linda was in the passenger seat, and Nina was in the back seat. They got hit by a truck at 11:20 AM. The girls were killed instantly. Linda was taken to the Albany Medical Center.

When we got to Harlemville on Saturday, Laura filled

us in on the some of the details. On Thanksgiving, Nina
and Kirsten drove to the Albany airport to pick up
Linda. Her plane was delayed, so they actually missed
Thanksgiving dinner at Laura and Stu's house. They
ate dinner when they arrived with Linda that evening.
Laura told us that after dinner, Nina lay on the couch
with her head in Kirsten's lap, and they talked about
their teachers. Nina stated that, if she had to choose
one teacher to have for every class, it would be Mrs.
Christiansen (the chemistry teacher whose class had
impressed me three weeks earlier).

Before they left, Kirsten asked to use Laura and Stu's
car the next morning to shop at the Salvation Army in
the nearby town of Hudson. There was some complica-
tion, but Kirsten was insistent and helped Laura figure
out a way to make it work.

Nina had a sore throat that night, so they went home.
Linda gave her a foot massage before bed. She still had
a sore throat in the morning, and Linda asked her if she
would rather stay at home and rest. No, Nina said, she
wanted to go along on the outing.

Somehow Kirsten got to the Summer home to get
the car and returned to pick up Linda and Nina. They
headed down Fern Hill, through Harlemville, and on
toward Hudson. Two miles from home, on a country
road overlooking the Catskills, a semi-truck was coming
up the hill toward them. Kirsten hit a patch of black ice.
The car went out of control and was struck by the semi.

No one was speeding. No one was under the influence of alcohol or drugs. It was merely that an inexpe-
rienced driver ran into some problems, which a more

experienced driver might have been able to control. Or maybe not.

A driver following the truck went to four houses before he found someone home to call 911. In the meantime, state troopers arrived on the scene. At that moment, Bob Elinson drove by, recognized the Summer's car, and continued home to tell Cecelia. Cecelia called the Summer's, got Stu on the phone, and told him Bob had seen his car in an accident, and then left for the accident site. Bob remained at home with Zusha and Sarah. On the way there, Cecelia passed Bruce Frishkoff walking along the road and picked him up. They arrived to see Nina and Kirsten still in the car.

Laura borrowed a car from the neighbors, and arrived just after the girls had been removed from the car in body bags. Karen Frishkoff arrived a few minutes later. The paramedics unzipped the bags for Laura and Karen to see them. In viewing Nina and Kirsten's lifeless bodies, Laura felt their souls hovering above the accident site.

Amazingly, within twenty to thirty minutes of the accident, four of the people who knew and loved Nina and Kirsten in Harlemville were there with them. This was comforting to me.

When I bring the accident scene to mind, I am filled with awe. I see Kirsten, flung out of her seatbelt into the back seat behind Linda, her head resting in Nina's lap. Still warm with the young and vibrant life that they had moments before been totally immersed in, they reflected in their death their love for each other and the acceptance of their shared destiny. The accident did not happen three weeks earlier when I was with them on the hectic freeway around New York City. It happened here, in a spot of majestic beauty, in a small spiritual community that could embrace and support them in their moment of destiny.

Linda was extracted from the car with the Jaws of Life and air-lifted to the Albany Medical Center. Nina and Kirsten were transported there in an ambulance. The 48-year-old truck driver was treated at Columbia Memorial Hospital in Hudson for back and leg pain. He had been hauling brewer's grain for cattle to a farm in Harlemville from Bangor, Pennsylvania.

Laura went home and made phone calls, first to the priest, and then to Dennis. The priest made suggestions to Laura as to how to help Nina and Kirsten in their transition, which she shared with Dennis. Cecelia made arrangements with the funeral home. Then, Laura and Cecelia drove to Albany. The Frishkoffs were already there and had seen Linda, who was about to undergo surgery for trauma to her face, arm, and pelvis. Now Bruce and Karen were in the morgue with Nina and Kirsten, reading from the Gospel of St. John to accompany them on their transition to the spiritual world. Laura and Cecelia also talked to Linda and then joined Bruce and Karen in the morgue.

Linda, though unable to speak, could vaguely communicate and was aware that Kirsten had died. She had hoped that Nina was still alive, but Laura and Cecelia told her the awful truth. Even though she seemed to be aware at the time, later in her recuperation Linda said she had no memory of the accident or the following days.

The girls remained in the hospital morgue overnight. Bruce, Karen, Laura, and Cecelia went home to be with their families and get some rest after a traumatic day. Although no one stayed with the girls, Linda's friends in California, for whom it was three hours earlier, kept up a vigil for them, reading from the gospels through the night.

The next morning, Nina and Kirsten were picked up and taken to the funeral home in Hudson, New York.

That First Night

That first night, I knew an exhaustion I had never known before. It was to become very familiar. For the next three days, my body bore the ravages of my emotional trauma. I longed for my bed hours before I could actually get to it.

For the next two years, I longed for sleep. Every night after dinner, my face began to ache with the aftermath of weeping. But because other parts of my life were going on as usual, I usually couldn't go to bed before 10:00, as there was always something that needed to get done after Soren was in bed.

This too, was a struggle—needing to take care of myself, but having a four-year-old and work commitments to fill my days. I had no choice in the case of Soren—he was my main responsibility. I chose to continue my two-mornings-a-week job as teacher of a parent-child playgroup the winter after Nina died, and then took a new preschool teaching position the following fall. I thought life should continue as usual. Looking back I realize I was in shock for a long time, probably about a year.

That first night, Dennis and I received an unexpected gift: a thinning of the veil between our world and the spiritual world. Upon awakening in the deep, dark night I felt a silent presence that both surrounded me outwardly and penetrated deep into my being. It was viscous, yet it was weightless. I did not want to move for fear it would go away. When I did move, I reached out to Dennis, and he was awake and listening in the silence also. We could feel Nina, or the angels, or God, right there with us. But as consciousness slowly returned, the wrenching pain of Nina's death took hold and coursed through us like poison.

Several times over the next few weeks, the heavenly beings visited me in the still of the night, flooding me with love and connection to my daughter. When the visits stopped, I wept in longing for that time not to end, for life not to go on as usual.

November 30, 1996

❋

Waiting

The next morning our kind friend, Victor, who had gotten our plane tickets for us, took us to the airport in his minivan. I have no recollection of how anything else got taken care of, like arrangements for the dog, the cat, the mail, our work, and Kevin's school. We would be gone for a week.

I did not cry on the way to the airport. I was numb. While waiting for the flight, I called the father of Nina's friend Lia in Kimberton, Pennsylvania, where Nina had been the weekend before. He had not heard the news. It was strange to be delivering such a message on a pay phone in an airport.

On the plane, Dennis and I sat together, with Kevin and Soren behind us. Observing this configuration, I was struck with the bleak realization that this was our family now.

Soren had been on an airplane once with me, flying to visit my mother in Indiana a year before. Otherwise, our family hadn't flown anywhere since we went to Hawaii in February of 1992, before Soren was born. Kevin loved flying. I had been fearful of flying before my trip to visit Nina three weeks before, but now I could sit calmly through the takeoff without breaking out in a sweat, which was a relief.

As we sat in the plane, Dennis and I took turns reading a passage by Rudolf Steiner that Victor had found for us. We were hungry for explanations. It was important for us to have something to grasp onto. The passage talked about the meaning of the death of a young person, particularly in a violent death. Through the experience of leaving the physical body suddenly, without preparation, Steiner explains that the soul has a direct confrontation with the forces of creation and dissolution, thus preparing it for a very creative future lifetime.

One of the pilots walked to the back of the plane and began chatting with us. He asked us why we were going to Albany. We told him that our daughter had died. He was sympathetic and said he would be praying for us. Strange that of all the passengers on that plane, he chose to chat with us!

After getting off the plane at around 1:00, a hospital van took us to the Albany Medical Center. It was a strain to be with the hospital staff driver who did not acknowledge what we were going through. Getting to the hospital and to Linda's room seemed to take a long time. We sat in a general waiting room until 2:15, then Dennis and I were led to Linda's room, while Kevin and Soren stayed in a private lounge.

We walked into Linda's room. She lay flat on her back, unrecognizable in her hospital bed. Her head was swollen out of proportion and was covered in bandages. Her left eye was bandaged also, and her right eye was closed. We approached on her right side and spoke quietly and hesitantly to her. She could hear us but could only respond by writing with difficulty with her right hand (not her dominant side). Her left arm and hip were injured, her left eye irreplaceably damaged, her jaw was broken, and her entire face had been rebuilt with metal plates in an 18-hour surgery through the night.

We told Linda about the pine coffins that were being made for the girls, about the plan for a wake, followed by cremation. Mostly we silently held Linda's hand to communicate our unspeakable shock and grief over the deaths of our daughters and the pain of her physical condition.

Two friends of Linda's, whom we did not know, were camped out in her hospital room. Larry Greenback and Carol Kinsche got news of the accident just before they were scheduled to depart on a trip to Mexico. They immediately flew to Albany instead. Larry, a medical doctor, acted as an advocate for Linda, and planned to stay with her for as long as was needed. I was extremely thankful that they were there. Thinking about caring for Linda overwhelmed me when all I wanted was to be with my daughter. Dennis' worry over Linda's tenuous condition and being there alone was relieved also.

After forty-five minutes, we left Linda to go downstairs to a cafeteria with Kevin and Soren to get something to eat and wait for Laura, who was coming from Harlemville to pick us up. We had been in Albany for two hours. I felt desperate to see Nina. It was taking forever, and we didn't know what was keeping Laura. We had no way to contact her. We had no control over the situation.

At about 4:00, Laura finally arrived. She told us that she and a friend had been to the funeral home in Hudson and had washed and dressed Nina and Kirsten.

I started sobbing. I wanted to be the one to do that! How could they have washed and dressed my daughter without me? Here I was waiting powerlessly in the hospital for three hours, longing to see my daughter, while she and a person I didn't even know were performing these precious last rites. Why had no one told me what was happening, or asked if I had wanted to be a part of it?

Through my anguish, I heard Laura say the funeral home staff had washed Nina's hair, which was full of glass shards, and had kept two thin braids in the front that Nina had made. Karen had chosen the clothing she would wear in her coffin. I asked about the clothing she had on at the time of the accident. Laura said someone had come in with the clothes that had been cut off of her and asked her if she wanted to keep them. Laura declined, as they were not in any shape to keep. This was also upsetting. I wanted to know every little detail of her life in the moment she died, and now I had no way to know. Not wanting to place blame on Laura, who was doing what she thought was best, I withdrew into my grief to endure whatever was to come.

We did not go to the funeral home to see Nina and Kirsten. Though I did not hear her say this at the time, Laura felt the funeral home basement might not be the best surroundings in which to first see Nina dead. She was trying to protect me.

Laura drove us one hour south to Harlemville, to get situated in her and Stu's home. We ate supper and put Soren to bed. Cecelia and Bob Elinson had offered to have the wake at their home. When Dennis had talked to Laura about these arrangements the night before, he had mentioned that the girls would have wanted the coffins to be the simplest pine box possible. A parent of a kindergartener at Hawthorne Valley School, who didn't even know the girls, offered to make them. The glue on the coffins had to dry before they could be brought to the Elinson's. This is what was delaying the girls' arrival.

Arrival

Finally, after 8:00 PM, Stu, Dennis, and I went to the Elinson's and found a house full of high school students waiting together. Flowers had already started arriving. We met many of Nina and Kirsten's classmates and friends. Each one had something kind and endearing to say to us. Several mentioned Nina lending them money, and commented that she would have been quite a bit richer if everyone who owed her money had paid her back.

The small living room with a hardwood floor was cleared for the arrival of the honored guests. Cecelia and Bob had pushed their couch, a few chairs, and a low chest of drawers against the walls. They put the flowers, candles, and photos of Nina and Kirsten on the chest. The coffins would lay side by side in the middle of the room, with space in between and on the sides.

As we waited, some of the students played music. Dennis and I were inspired to lead all these young people in a spiraling song and dance that we had learned at Camphill. "Spiraling into the center, the center of the shield, I am the weaver, I am the woven one, I am the dreamer, I am the dream."

It was very late when the girls and the coffins finally arrived, perhaps around 11:00. The young people respectfully went upstairs before Nina and Kirsten were brought in. First, several local fathers carried in the coffins. Dennis met the father who made the coffins and offered to pay him something for them, but he would accept nothing. This kind of graciousness happened all that week and for many weeks to follow.

Dennis helped to carry Nina on a stretcher from the mortuary hearse into the house. It was important for him to feel the weight of her body. Cecelia brought blankets and quilts to line the pine boxes. The coffins, placed on gurneys, were so deep that she kept bringing more blankets so the bodies would rest high enough for people to see. Finally we laid Nina in her coffin. We arranged her as best we could. Her head was wobbly. We thought perhaps her neck had been broken in the accident, but perhaps that is just the way a lifeless body is.

Friends of Linda and Kirsten, who had come from Boston, took care of Kirsten. She was almost too long for the coffin, so her legs couldn't quite be straightened out.

This all sounds matter of fact, but that's the way it felt. These were the physical circumstances we had to deal with. Our wills carried us in performing these duties, while our emotions were put on hold in this extraordinary situation.

We did not use any dry ice to preserve the girls'

bodies. The funeral director told us that because Nina
and Kirsten were young and healthy, their bodies would
not emit an odor during the three-day vigil. He recom-
mended keeping the room temperature in the low 60s to
help slow any decomposition.

Nina was laid on a sky-blue quilt. With her blond
hair and pale skin she looked heavenly against the blue.
Karen had gone to Nina's closet to choose clothes to
dress her in. There hung the white skirt I had sewn for
her birthday in October and an old white lacey peasant-
style blouse of mine. Nina had evidently worn these two
together on one occasion around her birthday. Karen
felt these were the most fitting clothes to dress her in,
which they were.

When I saw that skirt on Nina now, I was shocked by
the realization that I had sewn the skirt that was to be
part of her shroud. Her dress to lie in state in. Her death
garment. Her burial clothes. It was as if I had sewn her
bridal gown. Perhaps this was, indeed, the appropriate word for this outfit, for was this not, for Nina, like
a wedding? Perhaps she had found her life's fulfillment
in her union with the Divine. This was only the first of
many revelations, a hint of the great spiritual drama
underlying Nina's life and death.

Nina's long hair was flowing freely, with the two thin,
wispy braids starting at her forehead and going down
each side from the middle part. You could barely tell the
braids were there. Nina's body was amazingly unscathed
from the accident. She had a few small scratches and
bruises on her face and arms. This was puzzling and
hard to take. How could she have died such a violent

death while her body remained whole and intact? She looked peaceful and radiant. Kirsten, on the other hand, was obviously scratched and bruised around her face, and wore an expression of sternness or defiance.

I stroked Nina's hair, I stroked her face, I stroked her cold arms. Cecelia and I put a light blue sheet over her, up to her waist, so that she wouldn't seem so cold. I talked to her and loved her silently as I gazed at her. Candles were burning. Friends began to come downstairs and take turns standing at the sides of the coffins, greeting the girls in reverence. Some left little tokens or gifts on the girls' chests.

At 1:00 AM, Dennis and I finally got a ride back to the Summer's house. We left Kevin at the Elinson's to stay with Zusha and the other young people. He slept in Zusha's room upstairs, so felt like he was at the wake almost continuously. He probably got very little sleep or privacy, with people coming and going at all hours. A small group of friends sometimes went outside for time in the woods. For him and for all of us, this time had a dream-like quality, making it difficult to identify events and times exactly.

Dennis, Kevin, and I were exhausted, but events far beyond our control carried our family through the next two days.

December 1, 1996

✳

Sunday Morning

So much happened on this day, which seemed endless!
Dennis and I went to the Elinson's as early as we could,
which wasn't soon enough for me. I still had a desperate
need to be with Nina.

People arrived at the Elinson's all day long. Volunteers
came in shifts to be a constant presence with the girls,
silently reading or meditating. Local people came to pay
their respects, often parents with their teenage children,
many bringing a card or gift of sympathy to us. A few
people stayed a good part of the day.

Martina Mueller, Kirsten's painting teacher, sat by first
one, then the other, coffin, making a sketch of each of the
girls to give to Linda. We had declined someone's offer to
make a video for Linda, feeling uncomfortable with that
idea. This was the alternative way to bring something
visual from the vigil to her, to allow her the last look at
her daughter that she couldn't have in the flesh.

People from the Camphill Village in Copake, located
near Harlemville, came to the wake. Even though I only

vaguely knew them through our Camphill connection, I found much comfort in having these people present. We shared a basic spiritual foundation that connected us to Nina, who loved Camphill so much.

One friend from Camphill whom we knew a bit better, commented that the two girls lying in their coffins, one dressed in dark green, one in white, looked like a Prince and Princess. A few months later, back in Minnesota, another Camphill friend related a similar impression she had of Nina and Kirsten the previous year when they had visited Camphill. She characterized them as being like Snow White and Rose Red, the two fairy tale sisters who had contrasting temperaments. This friend had watched several young people walking in front of her house, Kirsten skipping merrily at the front of the group, while Nina contentedly scuffled along at the back. Both of these images were helpful for me.

On this day many of our relatives arrived. Stanley, Dennis' brother, had flown in with their parents, Harlan and Mildred. My brother, Alan, came by train from Indiana, where he and his oldest son had been for Thanksgiving. His wife, Andrea, and their two younger children drove from Boston to join them in Harlemville. My brother, Eric, was supposed to have come from Indiana with my mother, but had not been allowed on the plane because he strangely did not have a photo I.D. with him. My stepfather came with her instead, with Eric's suitcase!

When Alan, Andrea, and their three children arrived at the Elinson home, Dennis and I went out to greet them with hugs in the entryway. It was raining outside. As they removed their raincoats, we prepared the children for what was happening in the room. We wanted to make sure they felt comfortable seeing Nina and Kirsten. I tried to describe to them what Kirsten was like in appearance and personality, for they did not know her. I neglected to tell them that Kirsten had some scratches and bruises on her face.

They crossed the threshold into the candlelit living room, which was crowded with people, mostly teenagers. Andrea carried four-year-old Nevan, with seven-year-old Amelia clinging to her leg. Alan held the hand of nine-year-old Rylan. They came to Kirsten's coffin first. When the children saw an unfamiliar girl with scratches and bruises, they turned away, Amelia hiding her eyes against her mother, pulling her toward the door, and Rylan looking confused and clinging to his father. Alan and Andrea brought them back out to the entryway, explaining to us that they hadn't known that Kirsten would look like that. Dennis and I apologized and assured them that Nina would look like herself, with hardly any scratches.

My brother's family walked into the living room again, past Kirsten to Nina's coffin. When they saw Nina, Alan and Andrea started sobbing and, with tears streaming down their cheeks, they stroked Nina's flaxen hair.

Rylan and Amelia didn't cry; they just peered over the coffin's edge, right at Nina's face. They recognized their beloved cousin from a wonderful family visit a year ago, only now she lay still with pale glossy, almost glowing, skin. Years later, Rylan and Amelia told Dennis and me that the image of Nina is blurred with the other sensations in that room: brown wooden floors, wooden caskets,

wooden tables, the smell of candles burning, and wool wet
from the rain. They also remember the grey clouds that
hung over the entire weekend.

After ten minutes, Alan, Andrea, and the three children retreated to the sofa at the end of the room. Soon,
Rylan and Amelia ventured into the kitchen, where they
sat and visited with Dennis' parents, who were a calming
presence. Rylan returned to look at Nina several times,
touching her hair and hands, noticing new things each
time, and asking many questions about what he saw
and where Nina was right now. Amelia remained in the
kitchen, occasionally venturing to the door to peer into
the living room. Amelia also asked many questions about
death, heaven, and angels. Andrea and Alan answered
their questions as best they could while they sat on the
sofa, and later in the car. Nevan, the youngest, remained
in his mother's arms, quiet and subdued. He slept most of
the weekend and had a high fever the day of the funeral.
As Andrea said, "It was just too much for him."

Later that afternoon, when they returned to the home
where they were staying, Rylan and Amelia sat at the
kitchen table in front of the wood stove and drew pictures
for Nina and Kirsten. Alan brought the drawings to the
wake and placed them in the girls' coffins.

During the wake, my mother sat quietly in the living
room with her eyes closed. With her Alzheimer's confusion, it was a lot for her to take in. She was confused
all weekend. At one point, however, she walked over
to the coffin with me. For a few moments, we stood
side by side, arms around each other's waists. Mom
recalled some memories of Nina in total clarity. I have

no memory of this, but it is a poignant memory for Andrea. She remembers talking to me about it afterward, and that I was happy for the miracle of my mom being unexpectedly present with me at her first granddaughter's coffin.

All of these people were thrown together in the Elinson's living room. Dennis and I, and the others carrying the vigil, were doing what we needed to do for Nina and Kirsten, and everyone became a part of it. It was an amazing time. The event seemed to have an energy of its own, which enveloped everyone upon entering the house. Relationships were lifted out of their normal patterns and were acknowledged only in relation to what was going on in the room, which was a cosmic event. In this way, I felt connected by love to everyone there.

Poetry, Art, and Music

Christy Barnes was one of the local people present on Sunday. She and her husband, Henry, were two of the elders of the Harlemville community. Nina and Kirsten had cooked their meals for them on alternate evenings for the three months that they had been in Harlemville. Christy was an English teacher, a writer, and had published a book of poems and essays entitled *The Up-Rising in Dying.* In her 90s, she was petite, white-haired, rosy-cheeked, and dignified in her wool skirt and silky blouse. On Sunday morning she read out loud some of the verses for the dead by Rudolf Steiner included in that book. Two of them, from the perspective of the one who has died, became very meaningful for me.

In radiant light
'Tis there I feel
The power of life.
For death
Has wakened me from sleep—
From spirit sleep.
Oh, I shall be
And do from out me
What radiant power
Within me shines.

I was united with you,
So remain united in me.
Together we shall speak
The speech of eternal being.
Together we shall act
Where the results of the deeds are at work.
Together we shall weave in spirit,
Where human thought is woven
In the Word of eternal thought.

These verses helped me elevate my thoughts around this tragedy and not become mired in grief. I felt as if Nina was speaking to me as a spiritual being.

Christy sat on the couch writing poems about Nina and Kirsten on her pink miniature memo pad. She shared her impressions of Nina, which meant so much to us. She told us that Nina was cooking one evening and was visited by a spider. Without hesitating, she picked up the spider in her hands and gently set it outside. Christy wrote of this little incident in a poem reflecting Nina's down-to-earth, unflappable nature. Christy also recognized that our daughter was deep and wise.

NINA DIETZEL
by Christy Barnes

Nina, you carry us all in your heart,
And bring us together so we may not part.
You fill us with thoughts
That can nourish the soul,
And heap food in each bowl
Until healthy and whole.
We can follow your feet
To a practical goal.
You're at home with rough weather
And spiders and snow,
And smile on our ways
Wherever we go.
Deep in the wise, silent center of you,
You shed love and strength
On all that we do.

Even though Christy only knew Nina for a few months, she captured several aspects of Nina that were familiar to us. I smiled as I thought of how Nina worked with concentration in the kitchen, confident in her cooking abilities, and thorough in cleaning up. I thought of her tough bare feet, her feet in clogs, in hiking boots, and in Sorrells, and all the paths she had trod in her life. She was a sturdy girl with dauntless enthusiasm for the mundane and the adventurous. I was proud of the person she had become.

Channa Seidenberg came to the wake later that day. Channa is a lyre player, singer, and composer connected to Camphill Village-Copake. I was happy that she brought her lyre, for it was beautiful to have quiet music playing in the room with the girls. It also gave me a chance to sing, one of my great loves. Channa knew many Camphill songs, and it was comforting to have something familiar to focus on.

After singing, I was very tired and asked for a place to take a nap. I did not want to leave the house and go back to the Summers'. I just needed a break. While I lay on the Elinson's bed, the singing continued on in me. All of a sudden, I was thinking about songs I wanted to have sung at the funeral on Monday. One song wafted into my consciousness with special meaning. "The Jagged Hawthorne," taught to us by Lois Smith at Camphill Village Minnesota, was performed every year at the Whitsun (Pentecost) Festival. Nina, Gwyneth, and Annamaria, dressed in white, were the three main singers. The song used the metaphor of the white blooming hawthorne tree as the bridal veil of the earth awaiting its union with the descending holy spirit. I heard it now as their signature song, a crucial piece in their preparation for this moment of Nina's spiritual wedding. Her gown had been sewn months earlier, and the time for the wedding had come. She was truly radiant.

This was the first time that I had thought about the funeral, having been consumed by the emotions of the moment. Now I was anticipating this event with a creative rush, wanting it to be beautiful and meaningful, as if it were Nina's wedding. At the same time, as

I lay on that bed with Nina's body in the room downstairs, the fact that my only daughter would never have an earthly wedding catapulted me into sobbing in grief and disbelief.

Endless Day

This Sunday was the first day of Advent and the day of the Advent Garden, the festival our family celebrated at Camphill. In the late afternoon, Laura and Stu were taking their children to the Advent Garden at their home-based playgroup (preschool). We took this time away from the wake to go with Soren to the Advent Garden with the Summers. We did not want him to miss this beautiful festival, and we needed to be with him there.

Soren joined the group of eight children who sat together while Dennis and I sat at the back of the hushed room holding back tears as we watched. Each of the children walked to the center of the evergreen spiral to light their own candle, held in an apple, then placed it on the outward path amidst the others. Achingly, we watched the tender journey of each child with our daughter's life journey foremost in our minds. The inward and reflective mood in the semi-darkness was transformed as the light in the room grew with each candle added to the garden, illuminating our souls and the world. When all the children were finished, the teacher gently asked if I wanted to walk the spiral, but, feeling too vulnerable, I shook my head "no" and broke into tears.

We learned later that back in the Twin Cities, the Waldorf community had gathered on the same afternoon for their Advent Garden. Many of Nina and Kirsten's Waldorf classmates came to the Minnesota Waldorf School for this event and shared the struggle of coming to grips with their sudden deaths.

We took Soren home to the Summers' house. After he was in bed, we talked with Franziska Steinrueck, the Christian Community priest who would be officiating at the funeral for Nina and Kirsten. She happened to be in the area at the time, substituting for the local priest who was away. She told us she had intervened at the hospital to prevent the girls from having an autopsy. For that, Dennis and I were very grateful, because an autopsy requires cutting the body open to remove, weigh, examine, and dissect the organs, an invasive procedure that was totally unnecessary. We knew that Nina and Kirsten had no drugs in their system, and we didn't need to know the exact details of how they died. We preferred to allow their bodies to rest in peace.

This evening, Franziska wanted to hear about Nina's life so that she could deliver a eulogy the next day. Dennis and I were happy to have this opportunity to talk about our daughter.

We asked Franziska if we should take four-year-old Soren to see Nina's body before the funeral. We were unsure, for the playing he was doing with Kelsa and Martin, the Summer children, seemed to be good for him. At the wake there were mostly adults present. It would be hard for us to focus on him if he were there. She suggested that, in this situation, it might be a difficult experience for him to see the lifeless body, and that if he did have a strong inner need to see her, he would let us know.

We let Franziska be our guide, and gave Soren several opportunities to express an interest in seeing the girls, but he didn't. Mostly he had lots of questions at bed-time, like, "Do Nina and Kirsten still have legs?" and "Are their hearts still beating?" For several nights I told him the story of Nina, the sister who was overjoyed when he was born, who loved him and had played with him since he was a baby, who went away to school with her friend Kirsten, drew pictures and wrote letters to him, and now had gone back to heaven to be his special angel, forever watching over him. This seemed to satisfy Soren.

After talking with Franziska, I was exhausted, but needed to go again to the wake. There were several friends scheduled to arrive yet that night. Indeed, Patrick and Diana O'Brien, who had spent some time in the hos-pital with Linda, finally came to the wake after picking up Molly from the airport. Molly had gone to France for her 9-month stay the month before, but felt that she needed to come back for Nina and Kirsten's vigil and funeral.

Molly and Diana now could take care of Kirsten, decorating her hair with flowers, and softening the stern look. Karen had a hard time finding the appropriate apparel for Kirsten. She had chosen a green linen shirt with a high collar and a long skirt. No one recognized the green shirt (I think it was Nina's) or thought Kirsten looked like herself in it. She would have appeared more familiar in her favorite frayed thermal shirt!

Soon our Minnesota friends arrived, including Marianne Schneider, one of the first people we met in Minnesota, eurythmist and founding teacher of the Minnesota Waldorf School. She now lived in Camphill

Village Minnesota and brought Ciaran Leighton
(younger brother of Gwyneth and Annamaria) with her
from the Village. Annamaria came from Arizona, where
she was attending Prescott College.

I was touched and grateful that these friends came,
knowing that there were many more who would have
liked to come. Gwyneth, for example, was in England
for the year and could not make the trip. Dennis and I
received her sister and brother like our own children,
helping Annamaria and Ciaran through moments of
timidity. Crossing the threshold from the entryway into
the living room was the biggest challenge. I noticed
Annamaria's hesitation, went over to her, took her by
the arm, and led her to Nina's coffin, saying, "Let's go see
Nina." I knew she needed support to see her best friend
lying in her coffin.

December 2, 1996

Final Goodbye

This was the last day that I would be able to see my daughter in the flesh. Again, it was hard for me to be patient with morning rituals with Soren before going to the Ellison's. It was taking too long. Finally, I decided to go on foot, getting a much needed walk, as well as a head start. It was refreshing to be walking down the country roads. It had been raining and cloudy the entire weekend. The gullies beside the roads were flowing with excess water. At least it had stopped pouring for the moment.

When I arrived at the wake, there were not many people there. I went to Nina and talked softly to her, telling her goodbye from Soren and friends who could not be there. I unwrapped her Christmas presents from Kevin and Ciaran with tears running down my cheeks, telling her about them as I did. I lit the candles they had gotten for her. I stroked her arms, face, and hair, feeling as if I just couldn't get enough of her, hysteric that she would soon be gone from me.

More people arrived. Many of the relatives who were there the day before were back, including my mother and stepfather. My brother Alan came without his wife and three children. Alan and Andrea both had anxiety about this last time to see Nina and the moment of closing the coffin, so decided that Andrea would stay home with the children until the funeral. The high school students were noticeably absent. They were at school, practicing with the choir for a performance at the funeral that afternoon. I took a break in the kitchen and one kind soul massaged my back.

Harlan, Dennis' father, arrived with a poem that he had written overnight. Standing in the living room again, I noticed that sunlight was streaming through the windows. I went to the kitchen to find out the time. It was approaching 11:20, 72 hours after Nina and Kirsten's death. It had been cloudy and rainy all weekend, and now the sun was shining. I was filled with wonder. What a glorious moment this must be for Nina, a joyful release into spiritual existence. People began to circle around the coffins as the sun poured in through the windows. We did Halleluia in eurythmy, led by Marianne Schneider. We sang many songs. We read poetry, including the one written by Grandpa Dietzel.

As I thought—
about you—Nina and Kirsten—
Where did you go??
As I searched the SPIRIT
Love assured me that you
Will always be in my heart!

And as I lay down to rest
I fell asleep—and dreamed
I went to where all Love is:
And I saw a beautiful garden
Of flowers—
I was told to pick
All I wanted—
I picked two
And when I awoke
Those two beautiful flowers
Were still in my hand.

Impulsively, I took a bouquet of roses and handed them out to Kevin, Annamaria, Ciaran, Molly, and the other young friends who were there. We gave the roses to Nina in her coffin. Diana was doing the same for Kirsten. My hysteria had left me, and I was filled with a joyous peace. I was almost ready to say goodbye.

At 12:00, the high school students returned and new guests arrived, including some of my aunts and uncles. The priest performed the first half of the funeral. After words to the people gathered there, and prayers for the departed, she sprinkled Nina and Kirsten with holy water from a small vial. Some of the men present then lifted the lids onto the coffins. This dreaded moment felt right to me. The entire weekend of saying goodbye to Nina, the sunshine blessing the end of the three days since the accident, and the ritual performed by the priest, led me to acceptance. While Diana and Molly, who had not had as much time with the girls, were still wailing as Kirsten slipped from their view, I felt strong in my hard-won peace.

Dennis also felt this acceptance and readiness to move forward to a practical task at hand. He had screws and a cordless drill from the man who made the coffins. He began attaching the lids to the coffins, driving the screws into the predrilled holes. Alan passed screws out to involve other mourners. They would place their screw in one of the remaining holes. Then Dennis would drive it in as they watched. Alan's anxiety was eased by Dennis' comfort with what was going on, and he wanted to help Dennis' mom and my Aunt Lovina feel comfortable also.

When the lids were attached to the coffins, Dennis and Kevin, Stu Summer, Alan, Patrick O'Brien, and Bob Elinson carried the coffins out to the funeral home hearse to be driven two miles to the school for the second half of the funeral at 2:00.

Our family went to the Summer home for lunch and to change clothes. Kevin remembers that this was the first time he cried since hearing that Nina had died. After he had eaten and changed his clothes, he went outside by himself to the bushes at the edge of the yard and opened the floodgates, letting out the grief that had built up over the past three days. He said that after that first cry, he was changed. From that time forward, he allowed himself to tear up whenever he felt emotional at a movie, concert, or play.

Funeral

The Hawthorne Valley School festival hall was filled to overflowing. On one end sat the entire high school, faculty and students, who would be singing. Nina and Kirsten's coffins were close to the south wall, with the priest and two servers in their vestments and the musicians sitting near them. The rest of the mourners sat facing them, including Dennis, Soren, Kevin, and I in the first row. Many of our relatives sat around us. Two sets of aunts and uncles and a few cousins had arrived from Vermont, New Hampshire, Massachusetts, and Maryland.

Soren sat on Dennis' lap. He had many questions about the coffins, and wanted to make sure he knew which girl was in which coffin. Nina's coffin had an iris sitting atop it, and Kirsten's had a rose. Some of their artwork was on the wall or in the foyer.

What I remember most clearly about Nina and Kirsten's funeral service was the music. The high school choir sang selections from their current repertoire, including "Summertime," especially for Kirsten, who had enjoyed singing this piece in her History of Music class. They also sang the beautiful "Lacrymosa" from Mozart's Requiem, pulled from past repertoire and, at Dennis' request, a song they had learned just that morning. It was a German round that we sing in our family, "Alles ist eitel, du aber bleibst, nur wenn du ins Buch des Lebens schreibst" ("All is in vain, you only remain, when you have written in the book of life") and it was one of those songs that brought tears to Kevin's eyes. Channa Seidenberg played the lyre and sang "The Jagged Hawthorne" with Annamaria and another woman, just as I had hoped.

I felt surrounded, and not at the center of attention, at the funeral service. Surrounded by the beautiful music and the loving and striving thoughts of all those people, I felt honored, honored by all that love and honored to be Nina's parent. I felt proud and strong. I was grateful for the strength that was carrying me through these times. I never knew I had the strength in me, yet at the same time I knew that I myself had created, through my own spiritual striving, the strength that was now there for me to lean on. It was literally holding me up.

Some people left when the formal funeral service was over and the coffins carried out, but most stayed and moved chairs to create a circle. This was a time for informal sharing and offerings. Zusha and Seamus first played the "Ashokan Farewell" on the string bass and guitar on this occasion. I had never heard it before and was struck to the core by its simple beauty. This soulful tune became a theme song for our family in the coming months and years.

A mother from Harlemville spoke about a warm September Saturday when she met Nina and Kirsten walking through the farm fields bubbling forth in song. They were unabashedly singing Christmas carols. Later that evening, they continued singing them at a party at her house, including all their friends in singing "Angels We Have Heard on High." Then all in our circle sang this jubilant song with its drawn out gloria's, a powerful moment that left a lasting impression on Amelia (Nina's 7-year-old cousin) and probably many others.

While the funeral was going on, a local harpist hired by the Frishkoffs, sat beside Linda in her hospital room playing music so that she would be bathed in its healing vibrations. Afterward, high school students who attended the vigil, funeral, and memory circle went to the Albany Medical Center with instruments and voices to share with Linda some of the music, poetry, and words from the three gatherings she hadn't been able to attend. This meant so much to Linda. It was her lifeline to where she wanted to be and gave her a deep connection to many of the young people in Kirsten's life, which would nurture her in the months and years to come.

So many thoughtful things were said about Nina and Kirsten and the impact of their presence upon individuals and the school. We knew that we would have a very special relationship to this community far into the future. It felt magical.

We said goodbye to most of the relatives when they left the funeral, for they had to travel back to their homes and go on with their lives. My mother and step-father were being transported to the airport then, also. As I said goodbye to my mother, I was sorely grieved that I could not quite connect with her. She looked like my mother in her familiar maroon herringbone Pend-leton wool suit, but her rational mind was not all there, and I wondered what sense she was making of it all. This was a sadness that I could not attend to for a long time, for my present grief overwhelmed all others. I wanted more than anything to be embraced and comforted by my own mother, but all she could say were things like, "That was a nice service, wasn't it?" (as if it were any church service) and "Soren sat nicely through the service." She was not relating to me and my loss, or her loss. I had already lost her, as well.

This special mother-daughter line was broken, for I was an only daughter who had lost her only daughter.

The Week in Harlemville

✳

Nina's Room

On the Tuesday after the funeral, we went to the Frishkoff home for the first time. Everything else had been too pressing before then. We had said goodbye to our daughter, publicly and privately, and now we were approaching her space away from home. It was a holy moment.

We knew that Nina's bedroom was just as she had left it on a morning like any other. She had gotten ready to go on an outing, not knowing that it would be forever, that people would see who she was by how she had left her private space.

I had not been in this room since my visit in November. Some things were familiar to me—the India bedspread artistically draped from the ceiling above the head of her bed, the table from Kirsten beside the bed, and the stained glass piece hanging in the window. It was so sweet to see them again. I pointed them out to Dennis and his parents and brother, glad that I knew something about them.

What was different were the traces of Nina from the days before she died. These we discovered together.

There were some worn clothes slung over her chair.

There were her red plaid pajama pants draped over her pillow.

I picked up the thick blue wool sweater that Gwyneth had knit for her. I pressed my face into it and cried. This moment was almost more difficult than seeing her dead body. It was so hard to comprehend that Nina would never wear these clothes again. These fragments of her life were all we had left.

There was her backpack, filled with notebooks, unfinished schoolwork, pens, and pencils.

There, on the floor beside her bed, was a book set upside-down waiting to be picked up again.

I looked at this small book. It was entitled *None to Give Away*, inscribed to Nina on her birthday by Annamaria: "Dear Nina, All the best for your 18th year. Maybe a ranch in Montana won't be just a dream—someday—it might be real." Painfully I felt all of Nina's girlhood dreams come to naught.

There, on the desk, were two unfinished letters written by Nina. One was a birthday letter to Annamaria:

So we're both eighteen now! It is strange isn't it? I always rather dreaded this time when I would have to think about going out into the world and leaving my childhood behind me. But now that I've sort of moved on already and because everything changed anyway, it no longer seems terrible. God, sometimes I wish that nothing had changed more than anything, that we were all back in

*MN tucked cozily into our little sheltered community . . .
but alas, we're not.*

*Already, I miss this year. That sounds very silly and
sentimental but it's true. In a comforting way that I've
always longed life to be – this is perfect. I am going to a
Waldorf school, have a delightful class, a wonderful circle
of friends to do stuff with, I'm living in the country – the
list just goes on. I don't truly want it to go on forever but
it's just really ideal and I know that in the future I shall
often wish it were back.*

The other is a letter to "my dearest darling Molly,"
dated November 27:

*It is terrifying, isn't it? To go miles away from home and
everyone that you know and to find that you love them
all so desperately that it hurts and tears only bring
more pain.*

*Tomorrow Kirsten and I will try our luck once again at
getting to the airport to pick up Linda! We now have the
added excitement of icy roads on top of everything else
we can't do!*

The thoughts that Nina penned to her friends in the
last days of her life painted a picture of her inner being
at the brink of adulthood: full of confidence and love of
life, yet aware of her own vulnerability, and discovering
the intensity of her emotion. She was a delicate flower
just beginning to blossom and give herself to the world.

I just wanted to be in this room, smell it, feel it, touch
it, and leave it just like it was, always. It was not messy,
like her room often was at home between cleanings. It

revealed the habits of the independent person she was becoming, her simplicity, clarity, and artistry. It gave me the feeling that she had died in complete honesty and purity with nothing to hide.

Kevin had spent Monday night at Camphill Copake with Annamaria and Ciaran, who were staying with friends there. He joined us Tuesday evening. Dennis, Kevin, Soren, and I spent the last four nights of our time in Harlemville in the Frishkoff home. The boys slept in the downstairs guest room and I slept in Nina's bed. I claimed this privilege as Nina's mother, desperately needing to hold on to what was left of the physical connection to the child I had birthed.

There, I wrote a note to Nina, expressing some of the feelings surging through me.

Dearest Nina,

Sitting in your room under your canopy of love, I want to live in your life for days and days and days while it is still alive—before your towel and sheets are washed, while the scent of you lingers on all that you touched—I want to relish you for as long as ever I can before the memory of your body, your gestures, your joyous spirit grow dim— look at the views that your eyes took in, walk the paths that your feet walked.

Oh, will I ever stop worshipping the ground that you walked on?

Can anyone else ever be as sweet to me?

I was tending to the needs of my own grief, embracing the threshold that Nina had just passed through, immersing myself in her being as she was when she left us, thereby connecting with her spirit hovering over all that was hers.

Packing Away

We spent the following days visiting people and going through Nina's room. We needed to pack everything to send home to Minnesota. While Ciaran went home to Minnesota, Annamaria stayed longer and came to share this bittersweet task. I felt grateful to have her help me determine, from a close friend's perspective, what was important to keep and what wasn't.

As Annamaria and I sorted through Nina's clothes, she took what had special meaning to her and her sister. With difficulty, we threw away a few things that didn't hold any nostalgia. I felt especially attached to a few old t-shirts, the sweaters we had just bought before she left for Harlemville, her favorite green corduroys, and especially her shoes. They were dear to me, for they held the shape of her wide, solid feet, which had carried her through her life.

One afternoon we invited friends from the 11th and 12th grades to the Frishkoff house to spend time in Nina's and Kirsten's rooms. It gave us another chance to meet individuals and make connections with them. We offered some of Nina's belongings to them as mementos. I felt that Nina would have wanted them to be shared and not held onto. I kept only what was emotionally essential for me, a duffel bag full.

The O'Briens spent these days with Linda at the Albany Medical Center. We let the high school students be in Kirsten's room, but couldn't give them any of her possessions before Diana, Patrick, and Molly were able to go through them for Linda.

Kevin packed up Nina's stereo, which would now be his. We listened to the CD that was left in it. It was an Enya recording that Nina had either borrowed from Kirsten or acquired in Harlemville, for we were not familiar with it. We were spellbound by its haunting beauty, and because it was the last music that Nina had listened to. We found the soundtrack from *The Power of One*, which we had heard on the trip to Montana. It was one of Kevin and Nina's favorite books and movies. One chant on the soundtrack was more poignant now. We heard Nina's name in the African words, "Senze nina, senze nina . . ." from a funeral song for a young woman in the movie. We didn't know exactly what the words meant, but they pierced our hearts and became our family chant in moments of shared grief.

We also packed away Nina's artwork: the rose painting, the stained glass, Kirsten's table, and two clay figures sculpted only a few weeks before, kindly fired especially for us. We hoped UPS would carry all these precious things back to Minnesota safely.

On Nina's Desk

Nina's desk had two piles of papers on it: one with businesslike mail, mostly having to do with college exploration, and the other with personal correspondence, each letter neatly added to the top of the pile as it was received. This included our letters from home, birthday cards, and letters from friends, grandparents, and aunts. We were particularly struck by a poem written by Gwyneth.

BIRTHDAY POEM FOR NINA

I am greatly honored to be loved by Nina,
One who loves so freely, so honestly, without conditions.
She presents me with an image,
One of wholeness, of glowing beauty.
I can see her now,
As she pauses in her painting
To reflect upon her work.
Peering over her shoulder,
One can see Nina herself in the painting:
Her radiance, sensitivity, devotedness, and love.
Her friends mean all the world to her,
Without whom—she'd find life quite meaningless.
Perhaps she's unaware
Of what a blessing she is to us.
She's like a gardener to her friends;
Caring and gentle, she listens to each one,
Her presence like the soothing rain,
Her laughter is the sun.
I want to thank her with all my heart
For being who she is,
And for being who she is to me:
Because I love her.

What an affirmation Nina received from her friend. I was grateful that she heard these words before she died.

We added to the pile one unread letter which arrived after Nina died, a letter from her friend Livia from Saltash Mountain Camp in Vermont. Its arrival reminded us to notify these camp friends of her death. Nina would have seen one of them, Ruchama, on the Monday after Thanksgiving when she and Kirsten would have visited Middlebury College with Linda. Ruchama must have been wondering what happened to her visitor. That was a very hard call to make. We were sorry that we didn't call sooner to have given her the option of coming to the wake and funeral.

Ruchama later sent me a poem about my call to her and the missed visit. It captured the overwhelming feeling of grief and emptiness in the simple image of "the dining room you have never seen." It was a beautiful tribute to a friendship of three in a time of "fierce girlhood dreaming." I wished I could know this girl Ruchama, and her friend Livia, who would forever have a missing link in their threesome.

Nina's Journal

During these days, Dennis and I discovered Nina's journal. Sitting close together on her bed, we held the journal between us. The cloth covering of this 8½ x 5-inch book with lined pages had a floral print in shades of magenta and pale pink on an ivory background. First, we opened its pages and were overcome with the wafting scent of some sensuous incense or perfume that had become a part of the book.

On the facing page just inside the cover was an

emblem saying "This Book Belongs to:" and Nina had printed "Nina Christine Dietzel, September 1995– _____." That empty line after the dash felt like a dagger piercing my heart. We flipped to the back cover of the book. There she had written, "From Paul Bergh on my Christening Day, June 28, 1992."

Folded up between the front cover and the facing page were several sheets. We unfolded them each, slowly and gently: a notebook page of doodling by Fred, given away by the French words and handwriting at the top; a note from Ciaran expressing love and an apology for something that had happened that day; a book title, *The King of Children: A Biography of Janusz Corczak* by Betty Jean Lifton, noted on a small sheet; a love poem printed neatly in Nina's handwriting on two small sheets of rice paper; an anguished letter penciled by Annamaria, undated, but obviously written when she was in Ireland; a 16th birthday card made by Kirsten with a water color painting of a simple spotted maroon lily blossom on a blue/violet background; and a note inside that said, ". . . I love you so much Nina, and I treasure you as a flower treasures her beauty. You are my beautiful side."

But when we turned the first page, we saw something so beautiful that we read it again and again in disbelief, feeling time stand still. It was a formal dedication to Nina's journal, written in her most decorative lettering. Under a dried violet glued to the top of the page, the first line arched across the page: "Let this book of the flowers hold the essence of my Being." The remainder of the dedication was centered and went to the bottom of the page:

Let it hold in its bindings all of the passions of my youth.
Let it harbor the birth and renaissance of my
   inspirations.
Let the dreams that will inevitably fall over the pages
   of this book be blessed.
And lastly:
To they that find themselves drawn to this book—
Read it with freedom and let it be a joy to you!

What had been living in Nina's soul, that she would have begun this journal a little more than a year ago with an invitation for anyone who found it to feel free to read it, and moreover, that they should take joy in doing so?

Dennis and I took turns reading the rest of the journal separately, a very emotional experience for each of us. It revealed the inside story of the year that we had just lived through together. There was so much going on in Nina that we were unaware of. But Nina had invited us to read about her experience of that year. It was just one more thing that made us feel like she knew, on some deep level, that it was her destiny to leave us early, and that she was preparing for it. How generous it was of her to share her inner life with us on the pages of this journal!

Nina wrote about her "blanket of friends." Within this blanket there were four friends she described as her "pillars of sustenance and joy." These were Bethany Thorsen, "my beautiful flower child," Gwyneth Leighton, her "soul sister," Annamaria Leighton, her "wise sister," and Kirsten Bergh. Of Kirsten she writes, "If I were to be left with only Kirsten for the rest of my living days, I believe I could live a full life. I would mourn countless

others, and the world, but I feel that we have within us
all that we would need. No matter what comes between
us in distance or other elements, our bond shall always
be expanding. Even now, I feel it with each beat of my
heart." These two poems especially express the love
Nina and Kirsten had for each other:

Oh Kirsten, my Kirsten,
I want so badly for her to find what she needs.
Her soul is on some great and awesome mission and
She cannot fulfill it.
I give her all the power I can—
I would give her more if that were possible,
so intense is my love for her.
She takes it all in such grace,
Yet inside she battles and
Sometimes she shows me
a glimpse of that battle,
and she so needs to fight it,
yet so great are her everyday needs
that her powers are all used up.
So strong a woman is she.
I pray that she be held up
by all the loving spirits
that now hold her,
through her whole life.

I weep for the goodness of Kirsten.
Two souls sailing alone in a great sea
Were thrown together into the same harbour to rest.
She gave me the moon

And so have I given her the sun.
Now we dance forever in the moonshine
While sunbeams gently caress our cheeks.
It is all ours;
The crisp autumn mornings
with hillsides ablaze,
and crunchy leaves underfoot.

The depth of the expression of love Nina had for Kirsten overwhelmed our souls, as the images uncannily reflected where they were now, their bond ever-expanding into eternity.

Numinous

It was sad to reduce Nina's room to boxes and duffel bags. I thought it would also be sad for the Frishkoffs to have nothing left but a room that looked just like it did before Nina lived there. So I left her beautiful India bedspread canopy above her bed, even though it didn't quite match the bedding. It was a very representative expression of her ability to transform a functional space into something beautiful.

In this strange reality at the threshold, the mundane became sacred. I took home the Queen Helene deodorant, Kiss My Face Honey Calendula Moisturizing Cream, and Jason shampoo that were Nina's. She and I had bought new supplies of these items for her trip. Using them on my own body each morning became a ritual for me. Nina became more and more a part of me, as I applied layer after layer day by day. The hand

THE WEEK IN HARLEMVILLE

lotion and deodorant lasted an amazingly long time. It was more than a year later that I squeezed out the last drop. What was I to do then? How could I replace them? This was the struggle. The door to the threshold gradually closes as this monster called time comes between you and the event, and then the mundane must become mundane again.

The first time we revisited Harlemville, in June of 1997, Nina's bedspread canopy was still above the bed in her room at the Frishkoff's. The second time we returned to Harlemville, in June of 1998, the bedspread was gone. The same thing had happened for Bruce and Karen. Life had become normal again, and physical mementos no longer had the same power. A bedroom should look like a coordinated unit, not a patchwork of mementos. The power of the objects became disconnected from the things themselves; the power became internalized. Willingly or unwillingly, it seethed within, waiting to be released.

Singing

We planned to leave Harlemville on Saturday. On Thursday, Dennis, Kevin, and I attended a gathering held to bring our time there to a formal close and to come together as a community once more in honor of Nina and Kirsten. Channa Seidenberg played the lyre and Christy Barnes read some verses. The gathering was small and did not last long. In fact, Dennis, Kevin, and I felt it ended all too quickly. Kevin said to me, "Let's dance!" so we gathered round and tried, rather

unsuccessfully, to come up with a song and a dance that
went together, for no one had planned to bring instruments or call a dance.

Instead, we stood in a circle and sang many songs.
Because we were in the midst of the Advent season, we
sang Advent songs. Here, in another context, we experienced the power of community. The elders, middle-aged
teachers and parents, and youth all sang songs together
that they knew so well they didn't need song sheets. Seeing some of the young men singing earnestly as a part of
the community made a lasting impression on me. These
same friends played in Zusha's band. The new music
they created had its roots in this community singing,
giving them security and confidence to express their
creativity in new musical forms. Yet the community
singing still had power for them, too.

We took a part of the community home with us in
our hearts, and in a new song that we learned. It was
a simple Advent round, by Christoph Andreas Lin-
denberg, with a haunting, open quality, expressing the
struggle between dark and light at this time of year.

Oh darkness, oh tree,
You are like Advent,
Our companion
'Til light we see.

This is the time of year in which Nina and Kirsten
chose to take their light to the spiritual world, dispelling
darkness on both sides.

Coming Home

※

In Shock

Knowing that we would arrive home on Saturday, I thought we could stop at the Waldorf School's Holiday Fair on the way home from the airport. I went to this fair every year to buy holiday gifts and to stock up on craft supplies that weren't available anywhere else. Just in case I didn't make it there, I called a friend and asked her to do me the favor of picking up my favorite tissue paper and transparent paper.

When Dennis, Kevin, Soren, and I checked in for our flight at the Albany airport, we found out that our tickets were actually for Friday, the day before. Somehow, in our fog, we hadn't confirmed our flight or checked the date on the tickets. Thankfully, there was space on the Saturday flight, and we weren't charged any extra.

We were carrying Nina's ashes, which had been given to us in a metal box, in a small carry-on duffel bag. We set the bag on the conveyor belt to go through the X-ray machine, and the inspector lifting the curiously heavy bag off the belt asked what the contents were. Dennis said quietly that they were the cremains of our daughter. The inspector asked no questions and simply said respectfully, "Go ahead, sir." Dennis and I breathed a sigh of relief.

On the flight to Minneapolis, we thought that probably the most difficult week of our lives was behind us. We were returning home as a different family. The thought of Nina's empty bedroom, the empty chair at our table, the loss of phone calls and letters connecting us to our daughter, and our first Christmas celebration without her filled us with dread and emptiness.

As we arrived at the Minneapolis-St. Paul Airport, I realized that going to the Holiday Fair was out of the question. We were too exhausted to think about stopping by just to pick up a few items, which in any case would be impossible because of the many people we knew who would be there. Still in shock, I thought life would be going on as usual and I would be doing the same things now that I'd always done. My physical body and emotions told me otherwise. Nothing would be the same. Everything we did in this state of shock became emotionally traumatic, and therefore physically tiring. We had to learn over and over again to limit our activities to the essentials.

I often know what I need and am not afraid to ask for it. I knew that when we got home, we would want to have fires in our fireplace, so I had called and asked Michael to clean our chimney, a task due to be tackled this winter. I knew that I would want to have the house decorated for Advent, which I usually did the weekend after Thanksgiving, so I had called and asked two of my kindergarten teacher friends, Mary Lou Bala and Brenda Haak, to help me.

After arriving home and beginning to unpack, we built a fire. As we sat in the warmth of the fire's glow, our friend Christina Beck came to the front door with a huge basket of gifts from people at the Youth Initiative (Kevin's high school), as well as the craft supplies from the Waldorf School Holiday Fair. Then Christina, the administrator of the Youth Initiative, drove Kevin to "a party" at a friend's house in Minneapolis. This was an informal way for students to welcome Kevin home and be with him at this difficult time, helping to ease an awkward re-entry into the school community on Monday morning.

It was wonderful to start connecting with people in Minnesota, to share our grief with friends who were profoundly affected by Nina and Kirsten's deaths. Every night for three weeks, someone from Dennis' office or from our Waldorf circle came to the house with meals for us. That contact with people was very important. Having those meals proved to be essential. One night, there was a mix-up and no meal came. We didn't know what to do. The focus needed to get a meal together just wasn't there. With fruit, leftovers, cheese, and bread we made do that evening.

Advent Consolation

Our nightly ritual evolved spontaneously. After supper we built a fire, smudged the house, lit candles in the dining room, and turned off the electric lights. We lit the living room Advent candles in the wreath,

ceremoniously saying a special verse. Then Kevin lay
on the floor with Owintino, his black labrador retriever
dog. Soren put his pajamas on and snuggled up on
someone's lap or on the sheepskin on the floor with his
feather quilt over him. We sat in silence, or singing, in
front of the fire for a long time. We even let Soren fall
asleep and took him to his bed later.

This ritual seemed to fit everyone's needs. Kevin often
initiated it. I was glad that he was able to find a comfortable way to be with us and express his grief during this
time. I believe this was when he began to love part-
singing. It was a joy to have his bass added to Dennis'
tenor and my soprano, though we were painfully aware
of Nina's missing alto voice. We grew to love many of
the Advent songs we sang that year. Soren, to this day, is
always eager to sing during Advent, undoubtedly in part
because of the memories of closeness while singing as a
family in the weeks after Nina died.

Because Nina died at the beginning of Advent, we
already had rituals for the season that we built upon
to create a space to honor her and our grief. Advent
would never be the same for us again. It would always
be steeped in intense love and joy, pain and spirituality,
silence and singing.

Days with Soren

Dennis went back to work on the same day that Kevin
went back to school, the Monday after we arrived home.
He probably never questioned that he would do that.
After all, he was our provider. Perhaps he needed the

security of that identity to go on. His work, computer programming, required focus and clear thinking, and served as a distraction for him.

My main identity was as a mother. My very part-time work with the parent-toddler playgroup required preparation, imagination, and presence with little children. I couldn't even think about going back to it right away. A kindergarten teacher I spoke with in Harlemville suggested that I take a break from my parent-toddler playgroup until after Christmas. I welcomed that advice.

I spent my days at home with Soren. It was good to have the familiar routine of helping him get dressed in the morning, eating breakfast and lunch together, doing laundry, going outside to play, and reading to him at naptime. Much of the time that was not what I thought I wanted to be doing, but it probably saved me from wallowing in my sorrow.

I tried to meet some of my own grief needs in our activities together. I did not try to hide from Soren that I was grieving and sad. In this way I felt I also gave him the possibility of expressing his own feelings of grief. He was a child living in the moment, however, and did not dwell in sadness. He was action-oriented and ever playful. Whatever thoughtfulness I brought into our play together was taken up whole-heartedly by him, such as the activity described in my journal entry below.

Soren and I walked in the snowy woods, with me pulling him on the sled. I wanted to stop and be silent in the woods—but no, we had to play house. So we built houses in the snow. I made a nice seat in the snow and then wrote with a stick in the clear snow:

SIT AND REST
IN MEMORY OF NINA DIETZEL

Soren said at naptime, "If we keep smiling, our hearts won't stop beating."

Perhaps Soren was trying to cheer me up with that little gem. If we could keep on experiencing joy, our lives would go on, our hearts would heal.

We made a ritual of taking wilted flowers from the many arrangements we received to the woods to decorate the frozen memorial. We walked by it often, and wondered if other people stopped and wondered who had died. We could see that many dogs stopped by! Occasionally, the yellow snow was refreshed with a new layer of flakes. We watched the seat thaw and freeze again. For as long as the snow remained, far into February that snowy winter, our sanctuary remained in the woods.

One clear day, while playing in the snow in our yard, I was caught up in my own thoughts, not engaged in what Soren was doing. I began to trace giant letters in the snow with my feet. I wrote, WE LOVE YOU NINA, in a giant heart. I told Soren that I had written a message for Nina in heaven. We stood gazing into the blue sky, with our arms open wide, crying, "We love you, Nina," exuberantly, desperately trying to find her.

Words of Consolation

Sympathy cards and letters kept pouring in for weeks after we got home. I began to look forward to the time they arrived every day. I read them all and (with the inevitable tears) felt the sympathy of people who were impacted by Nina's death. People took it deeply, as if she was their own child. I began to realize how wide the circles were that Nina's life and death had influenced. The letters came from Europe and all over the United States, from long lost relatives and people in the Anthroposophical Society whom we didn't know personally, from Camphill circles, from Waldorf circles, and from Farm and Wilderness circles.

Dear Dennis, Dear Marianne,
To lose a child at any age is a shock, but to lose one in her teens must be almost unbearable. When we were in Thailand and our oldest, Steve, was born, we knew a fine older co-worker who had previously lost a grown son. I told him at the time I was afraid to love Steve so much, that if I had to, I could not give him up. He told me "to love him with all your heart" and you'd find a way, if that ever occurred. Now this has happened to you, and our love goes out to you, but you, too, can find a way.
   Relative

From what I know of Nina, it is clear to me that she was dearly loved by her family and able then to radiate that warmth and love out to others. When Nathan speaks of her, he uses words like kind, loving, sweet, gentle, generous. . . . So, I find myself wanting to thank you for bringing her up in such a way that those qualities were free to emerge and be shared with the world.
   Youth Conference Leader

While life around me goes on as if nothing had happened, I do know that something has changed, and that things are not now as they were before. Nina is no longer here, and so long as I am here, I will not see her again. But my life is more than just this moment. It is all the moments I have been and all the moments I will be. Nina is a part of it, and nothing can ever change that. The threads of our lives are forever intertwined. Knots, once tied in the web of lives, can never be untied, and paths that once crossed, are linked in all time.

It fills me with joy that Nina has become a part of my life, and I hope and pray to have given her something in return. I am deeply thankful to you for having been a home and a family in this world to such a beautiful being. May your strength and courage never fail you.

　Family Friend

The total summer conference group have developed very strong bonds which now have grown even stronger by Nina and Kirsten crossing the threshold, separating them from our physical senses. We are quickly coming to the end of an important year of new resolves and I feel that our two dear ones are extremely important to the whole of that wider age group which is seeking a connection to the spirit-world.

　Youth Conference Leader

Nina was so peaceful and happy when we last saw her. She probably has always had a calm presence; she seemed so mature, and genuinely happy about being in Harlemville and having the opportunity to go to

Hawthorne Valley. We are grateful that the experiences we've had of her and of her friendship with Lia were so recent and so heartwarming.
Camphill Friend

In the two+ hour gathering at the school on Sunday night, there was a movement from impressions of sense-less loss and tragedy to an assurance of the spiritual reality that there is no loss or pain in that realm, and all things shall be understood.
Waldorf School Teacher

How fortunate we are, in the face of such powerful sad-ness, to know of the powerful sunburst of light from Nina experienced by those across the Threshold.
Family Friend

It is as if (children who die at around this age) only need to get a glimpse of the life on earth in this particular time, which is necessary for work in other worlds or in a later incarnation. So they already have a complete-ness that normally is only achieved after a long life of struggles and striving and overcoming of weaknesses and obstacles. I am sure you will feel their presence and help in the times to come.
Family Friend

Rudolf Steiner spoke words of comfort in saying that those who die young have made a sacrifice and can bestow much on those who remain behind, giving strength, love and inspiration for our tasks on earth.
Family Friend

I have been filled, still each day anew since Nina and Kirsten's departure, with a much stronger call to cherish more deeply and sincerely each moment that I have with my kids. And I think everyone has received a tremendous wake-up call to take in, and be more present, for each other in all that we share and do together. These are such precious gifts, and only a few of what feels like a great and ever-growing bounty of others that these two young souls have blessed us with. In certain moments it has felt like they have sacrificed their lives for these gifts and blessings.

Family Friend

If we can give them one gift, it would be to let their deaths change our lives for the better. Concentrate on the times we spent with them and remember. Remember the incredible energy that Kirsten brought with her into everything she did, and apply that same energy to your everyday life. Remember the all-encompassing love that you felt flow from Nina, and spread that love to the people around you. If we can do one thing for them, we can emulate their best qualities to make the world a better place. Most of all, remember them, and when you are experiencing total joy, think of them, and let them be a part of that joy.

Youth Conference Participant

Many of the words that people wrote served a great purpose for us in creating a picture of understanding from many perspectives. Some people couldn't find words to write, but sent cards with beautiful artwork. All these gestures of sympathy enfolded us in a comforting blanket of warmth.

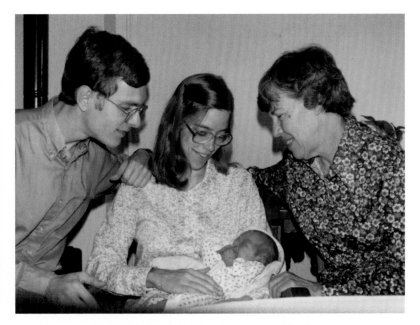

Oma visits Nina soon after her birth, October 17, 1978

Dietzel family, Indianapolis, Indiana 1982

Dietzel family at Maplewood State Park, 1988

Three generations, Spring 1990

Nina and Kevin with godmother, Laura Summer, 1986

Kevin, Nina (d.1996), Paul (d. 1995), Kirsten (d. 1996),
and Linda Bergh, Jan Zuzalek (d. 2009)

Nina, May, 1993

Nina in Ireland, summer 1995

Nina and Marianne, December, 1994

Oma and Nina, spring 1996

Serious, summer 1996

Inward, summer 1996

*Linda, Marianne, and Dennis at dedication of bench in
memory of Kirsten and Nina, fall 2001*

Baby Steps

On Friday, December 13, I was invited to the annual
kindergarten teachers' Advent gathering at Mary Lou
Bala's home. Kevin was invited to a sledding party at a
friend's house. I dropped Kevin off at the park where the
sledding was taking place, then drove on to Mary Lou's.
I knew several of the teachers gathered in Mary Lou's
living room quite well, others not so intimately. Most
of them I had not seen since my life was turned upside
down. As I walked in, I was awkwardly aware that my
situation was on everyone's mind. We were all new at
figuring out how to go on when such a dreadful event
has invaded peoples' lives. Of course, they wanted to be
supportive of me, and much of the meeting was devoted
to informal conversation.

In the course of the social time, "Santa Lucia" (my
friend Debbie) appeared before us, dressed in white
and wearing her crown of candles, handing out sweet
tea and buns. This was, indeed, Santa Lucia day, which
is traditionally celebrated in the morning in Waldorf
classrooms. I wondered if my friends had planned her
appearance at this evening meeting especially for me. I
had shared with many friends the beautiful Santa Lucia
tradition at Camphill. The white gown, the glow of the
candles, and the Santa Lucia song brought on a flood of
emotions. I could not hold back my tears. Santa Lucia's
appearance on that particular December 13 poignantly
evoked the memory of Nina and her two friends grac-
ing the Village as Santa Lucia and her attendants, and
the sadness that there is no longer a girl in my family to

carry out this tradition. Nina, Gwyneth, and Annamaria will be the Santa Lucia angels in my heart forever, even if a granddaughter comes along to play the part sometime in the future.

I left the meeting to return to pick up Kevin. I told another parent at his friend's house where I had been for the evening and said, "I feel like an adult again." I had accomplished the challenge of going someplace by myself, an ordinary activity for folks living ordinary lives. It reminded me of going "out" for the first time after the period of seclusion while recovering from childbirth and bonding with a newborn. I still needed to be in my cocoon and tend to my newborn and fragile self. Emergence into the world and normal life would come slowly.

Linda's Homecoming

Linda came home after a week in New York also, but her homecoming was quite different. She was flown via air ambulance from the Albany Medical Center Intensive Care Unit to Fairview Southdale Hospital in Minneapolis. Without husband or daughter to receive her, she was met instead by friends. A host of people came around the clock to be with her in her hospital room.

Linda's entire face had been smashed in the accident and had to be rebuilt with metal plates. Her left eye was removed, having lost all function, to be replaced with a glass eye. Her mouth was wired shut for six weeks to allow for the healing of her face. She had to be fed through a syringe. People brought healthy concoctions to feed her every three hours for several weeks. Linda also had a broken wrist and broken pelvis.

Our family first went to see Linda with a small group of friends to sing Advent carols to her on a Sunday morning. We took our turn feeding her. Linda was more alert now than when we saw her in the Albany Medical Center; however, talking was still challenging. Soren and his friend Rachael Pilgrim were totally fascinated with her method of eating with a syringe, and imitated her speaking with her teeth clamped together.

Being caught up in our own devastating grief, we were not involved in Linda's day-to-day care. A wave of people came to her aid, spending many hours with her, helping in a myriad of ways. Her injuries on top of the double loss of her husband and her only child drew people to her in sympathy and kindness.

Linda tried to walk after three weeks of laying in bed and felt like she was 95 years old. On the day of Nina's memorial (December 21), she was moved to Abbott Northwestern Hospital so she could have more intensive physical therapy. She wanted so much to come to Nina's memorial in her wheelchair, but realized that she didn't have the strength. Having missed all of the rituals for the girls in New York, she was pained at having to miss this, too. She began to plan a memorial service for Kirsten in the spring when she was recuperated enough to be there.

Memorial

❋

Friends

On Saturday, December 14, we opened our house to Nina's friends from Armstrong High School. Kevin was not at home—he was with his own friends. Dennis, Soren, and I welcomed five girls who showed up together at our door: Bethany, Cari, Shannon, Geri, and Alexis. We sat on the bed, on the extra futon, or on the floor in Nina's room. Soren climbed onto laps and snuggled, as if he sensed a presence that was like Nina, the big sister he liked to cuddle with.

I didn't know any of these girls, except Bethany; Nina had not spent much time with her school friends at our home. I found them all to be open, friendly, and expressive of their sympathy for us. Together we looked at Nina's clothes, artwork, and photos. We shared happy memories. We cried as we shared how we had learned about Nina's death. The hour and a half together was a sort of a pre-memorial service, a time to help these friends process what had happened, since they weren't able to be a part of the wake and funeral in Harlemville.

But it was not only for them. For us, it was an opportunity to make connections with a part of Nina's life that we were not so in touch with. It was wonderful to hear Geri, Cari, and Bethany talk about the last time they had with Nina—an evening at the Minnesota State Fair, defying the weight limits with all four of them in a cable car suspended above the fairgrounds. I asked Alexis about an incident Nina had shared with us: their being kicked out of study hall for laughing. Nina's telling of the story the year before had made me laugh so hard I had cried.

I remembered that during Christmas vacation when Nina was a junior at Armstrong, two or three of her friends came to the door with a bouquet of roses for her. She was delighted at the surprise and thanked them, but did not invite them in. I asked if any of the girls in this group had given that gift. They hadn't, but remembered that Nina had once said, "Everyone should receive a dozen roses at least once in their life." They knew the friends who had fulfilled this wish for her. Did these friends somehow know that Nina would not have much time for her wish to be granted?

Shannon mentioned a song on an Enya album called "Shepherd Moons" that she associated with Nina. She had just purchased the album when she came home to find out about the accident from her parents, who had heard it on the television news. She read the words of "Evacuee" to us—we did not have Nina's stereo there to play it. Dennis and I were touched by her sharing this with us. We were touched by the closeness all of these girls felt to Nina. We parted, vowing to keep in contact.

Elegy

Three weeks after Nina's death, we were getting ready for a memorial service for our daughter. What a strange thing to be doing during Advent. What a strange intrusion on people's lives it would be, to have a memorial to attend in the midst of last minute Christmas preparations and pre-Christmas celebrations. Yet what else could we do? Wait until after Christmas and pretend that the accident didn't happen and we didn't lose a daughter?

Several guests traveled to Minnesota for the memorial. Dennis' brother, Stanley, drove from Chicago with his wife and daughter, and stayed for the day. Dennis' parents drove from Indiana and stayed with Aunt Helen.

Rachel Wetmore, Nina's newly found friend from Harlemville, was sent by her class and others in the community to be the New York presence at Nina's memorial. We picked her up from the airport on Friday night and gave her Nina's room. Soren was quite taken with Rachel and attached himself to her at the memorial. They sat together through the entire service, except for when Rachel joined the Youth Initiative in singing the song, "Miserere."

On Saturday morning, my brother Eric, his wife Sherry, and their two boys, Seth and Aaron, arrived at our house exhausted from an early morning flight from Indiana. They had time to refuel before getting dressed and caravanning to Lake Harriet Community Church in Minneapolis. We were glad they were able to come, since they had missed the wake and funeral in Harlemville.

We arrived early at the church. Friends were there
to help set up memorial items in "The Garden Room." I
greeted them as they were arranging a table with colored silks and flowers, a collage of photos, an enlarged
close-up photo, and some of Nina's artwork. All of a
sudden it seemed so unreal to me, even though I had
spent the past two weeks planning the service, getting
Nina's watercolor painting framed, choosing photos
for the collage. Was this my daughter for whom all this
to-do was about? Did this really happen? Was all that I
had left of my daughter that earnest picture on the wall?
And where was she now?

Saturday, December 21, the day of the memorial, was
the day that Nina was scheduled to arrive home from
Harlemville for Christmas. Oh, what would it have
been like if she had arrived for Christmas, year after
year, with different stories of her life, of adventures and
misadventures? Perhaps it would not always have been
happy. Perhaps it would have been difficult. Perhaps
her spirit would not have flowered in this life and the
anguish would have been even more difficult for me.
Perhaps, in her death, she had more positive influence
on the world than she would have in her life. In the end,
we just don't know. We can only know that this was how
it went, and trust that this was how it was meant to have
gone. It couldn't have gone another way. In the end, we
can only love what is ours to love. That means loving the
grief and sorrow.

It means not being afraid to walk in that dark landscape, not being afraid to feel again how real death is.

Nina's friends, the ones who had come to our house,

and many more from Armstrong High School, came
to the memorial service. A string quartet, with Nina's
orchestra teacher directing, played twenty minutes of
beautiful classical music at the beginning, including
Franz Schubert's, "Death and the Maiden Quartet."

Laura Summer came from New York to be a part of the
memorial service. Annamaria, Laura, and Annamaria's
father David presented Nina's biography. Annamaria told
stories of her girlhood with Nina and especially of their
dreams about their weddings. Annamaria sensed, as I had
felt at the wake, that Nina's dream of her wedding was
fulfilled by her death. Laura talked about her most recent
experience knowing Nina as a young woman in Harlemville, leading up to Thanksgiving Day and the accident on
the following day. She brought the scene of the accident
to life in a spiritual way that was reassuring for the audience. David gave a spiritual perspective to the intertwin-
ing of the lives and destinies of Nina and Kirsten.

Kevin played a piece of music on his cello that he
had worked on the year before. It was Gabriel Faure's,
"Elegy" (a song expressing sorrow for one who has died).
I had accompanied him on the piano the year before,
but now his classmate Christine Worrall played it with
him. I knew the piece inside and out. The first notes, so
soulful and strong, rich and beautiful, made me start to
cry, but I closed my eyes and sought to find the space
within me where the music lived. I felt it rise up as the
song of Nina's life. As the music filled me, I let the music
rise up to her. It sang of a life lived with intensity, with
pain and tribulations as well as joy, but with a love that
transformed all into deep peace at the end. It was so

very fitting and brave for Kevin to play that piece, to walk in that dark landscape through the music, and to know that in the end, there is peace.

Gratitude

We were surprised by the many friends and acquaintances from our past, as well as unexpected relatives, who showed up for the service. Sitting in the middle of this throng of people, cradled by friends in front of and behind us, and looking to friends above in the balcony, Dennis and I felt profoundly supported and loved.

A time for sharing was included in the service, and many of Nina's high school friends spoke heartwarmingly of memories of Nina from working with her in *Fiddler on the Roof,* playing in the orchestra with her, or being in classes with her. They all felt inspired by the breath of fresh air she brought to their lives. One friend read a letter she wrote to Nina, saying that, while some people may cry tears for what should have been, she cried tears "for what was beautiful. . . . Hold my hand as I try to share a piece of you with those who did not feel the grace of your presence. Hold my hand as I finally offer you the love that I didn't recognize as such until your life was complete. I love you and I love every rainy day that you told me was beautiful."

Only one boy, who knew Nina from orchestra, expressed despair at such a beautiful life being taken. This prompted a response from Dennis' Aunt Helen, assuring the young people that faith in Jesus Christ offers hope for the despair.

My brother Eric spoke about the line of strong women in the family that was now broken. An old friend of mine from the Waldorf School, sitting in the balcony, read a poem she had written about Nina and Kirsten, "Sisters of the Wind."

The common songs, the Eurhythmy performance to a reading of I Corinthians 15, 51–55, the Youth Initiative choir, Kevin and Christine Worrall on the cello and piano, Sarah Worrall on the harp, and Stefan Orsak on the violin, all contributed to an uplifting spirit that was felt by all.

I was grateful for all of Nina's friends, for our friends and family, and the part they played in her life and in her death. At the end of the memorial service I spontaneously spoke my gratitude, concluding with, "You are all a part of her, and she is a part of you."

Christmas Candles and Roses

My brother's family and Dennis' parents spent Christmas with us. Rachel was to have returned home before Christmas, but she called her parents and requested to stay longer. She, Kevin, Seth, Aaron, and Soren fell into a happy affiliation. They stuck together like a litter of puppies, tumbling, playing, and napping as one bunch. Watching them laugh together made me happy. Nina had loved her cousins, Seth and Aaron, whom we had visited intermittently over the years. Nina and Seth were four months apart, and Aaron was a year younger than Kevin.

Eric and Sherry had never stayed at our house at Christmastime. In the days between December 21 and

Christmas, we carried out holiday preparations together. We baked Grandma Dietzel's cutout molasses cookies. We dipped beeswax candles for lighting on our Christmas tree. We polished Red Delicious apples, attached loops of carpet thread, and hung them on the tree. We folded tissue paper stars to decorate the windows.

Dennis and I hadn't done our Christmas shopping and didn't have gifts for the guests, so Sherry and I created gifts for everyone. We filled some antique crocheted rounds with potpourri and tied them up with ribbons. I also gave some of Nina's treasures as little gifts. Some were insignificant items left in her sewing basket, like bits of knitting meant for doll slippers that she never sewed up. Thank goodness I had purchased one gift in November, so that Santa Claus could make an appearance! On Christmas morning, a little pair of cross-country skis were under the tree for Soren. He loved the skis, but he was soon more absorbed in the candy and toys in his Christmas stocking and the big yellow Tonka truck from Kevin that he could play with inside.

We had simple meals. My brother and I went to the grocery store. For the 3½ weeks since Nina's death, I had not needed to shop since friends had delivered our meals. Planning meals and going to the grocery store took great effort, and I felt proud that, with Eric's support, I was able to do this routine activity again.

The weather got very cold, and it snowed every day for a long stretch, so the snow began to mount up. Eric took on shoveling the driveway—a thrill for a Hoosier who knows only an occasional snowstorm. The cold and snow contributed to the cozy and dreamy atmosphere of those days together. The kids went sledding both by daylight and by moonlight on a nearby hill at the Theodore Wirth golf course. Soren tried out his new skis on the small slope in our back yard, using them as a sled that he sat on, having great fun.

Several months before, I had bought tickets to a play with the thought of a family and friends' outing while Nina was home. We made it an outing, without Nina. It was fun for those who were from smaller communities to see a play in the Twin Cities—The Three Musketeers at Theatre de la Juene Luene. Dennis went, but I stayed home with Soren. I still didn't feel up to such an event. I needed to be with Nina, which meant reading and re-reading her journal and letters, sorting through photographs, and listening to her music after Soren was in bed. Even though the group activities were lovely, I found it hard to be social or to think about attending a play. I did not want to be entertained that night. I was in my own private world with Nina.

On Christmas Eve we shared our family's traditional ceremony with our guests. Gathered around the tree in our family room, we turned off the lights in the room and lit the beeswax candles adorning the tree while singing our most beloved Christmas carols. This year the tree had the special addition of real red roses (a gift from the Miller family) placed in the branches. The golden beeswax, the shiny red apples, and deep red roses amongst the evergreen boughs lit by the candles' glow created an image of radiant beauty that filled our souls on that dark winter night, a Christmas made more beautiful by the underlying sadness and mystery that united us all.

Ministered to by Angels

After all the company departed, but while still in "Christmas vacation" mode, I tried going after-Christmas shopping. I usually found time each year to "shop the sales." This year I went to a small shopping center with a friend. I held up for an hour or so of looking through racks of clothes, but then I felt too tired. We went to a small deli for something to eat. The clamor of voices, music, dishes and silverware, the lights and unnatural environment, the people rushing around, the commercialism—it all contrasted too much with the sacred inner world I was living in. Caught off guard again, I thought I could do "normal" things, but found out I couldn't.

The next time I went to a shopping mall was a month or two later when I needed clothes. I was filled with sadness at not having Nina to go with me. She was the only one in the family who went shopping with me. Actually, we were usually shopping for her. We always visited the same sequence of our favorite stores. I planned to go to these same stores. As I walked toward the mall entrance, I began to feel that I was not alone. Nina's being was present with me. I walked into the mall and found a bench to sit on. I closed my eyes and cried silently. I could have sat there all night in that sweet halo of her being while the world rushed by me. I felt as if I were kneeling in a church, being ministered to by angels. However, after five minutes, I realized I couldn't sit there endlessly. I got up and went on with my shopping, with Nina by my side the whole time.

Nina accompanied me for several more shopping trips to two different malls where we had shopped before. These experiences gave me confirmation that I must go on living in the materialistic world, and that the spiritual could penetrate it. They also assured me that Nina truly was with me in her new state of being. What I didn't understand was how or why she chose the times she did to make her presence known, and whether or not my own state of soul had anything to do with it. Lacking understanding, I accepted the visits as precious, extraordinary gifts that were meant especially for me and validated our mother-daughter relationship.

Dreams

✻

Before Christmas, one of my friends gave me a dream journal entitled *The Thirteen Holy Nights: A Festival of Inner Light to Birth the Spirit Child.* It was a guide through the days between December 25 and January 6 (Christmas to Epiphany) when the veils between heaven and earth lift, opening the human being to insight and growth. Listening to one's dreams during these thirteen nights helps in sensing one's emerging inner birth and the potential of the year to come.

Still enfolded in the closeness of the spiritual world that Nina's death brought about, I wanted to be vigilant to whatever messages might be coming to me at this spiritually auspicious time. With Soren appearing at my bedside to wake me up every morning, it was a challenge to remember my dreams. I tried to pull him into the mood by letting him draw a picture while I drew or wrote an image from a dream, a mood of soul or feeling that I awoke with, or thoughts about the previous day.

Second Holy Night

On this night, I didn't have an actual dream, but was struggling with misgivings over serious conversations with Nina. I remembered the pained look on her face at these times. In my sleep, the image of Nina crowned with a wreath of flowers came to me with a feeling of forgiveness from her.

Third Holy Night

The evening of the third Holy Night, Dennis and I sat in a sauna with our friends. I reflected on all that I had been called upon to do as a mother that day, putting aside my own grief needs. The sauna lifted my grief for a brief time, opening me to lovemaking with my husband during the night, but even that I could not experience isolated from my absorption in Nina.

Fourth Holy Night

During this night I experienced Nina and Kirsten as spiritual beings, bathed in color and light, enveloped in the "music of the spheres." I felt the contrast of their elevated existence with our material existence on earth. From their perspective, even our thoughts of them seem heavy and dense.

Fifth Holy Night

Our family visited the Leighton family at Camphill Village Minnesota at this time. Upon entering their living room, I was astonished to see several enlarged photos of Nina that I had never seen before. Gwyneth had taken these

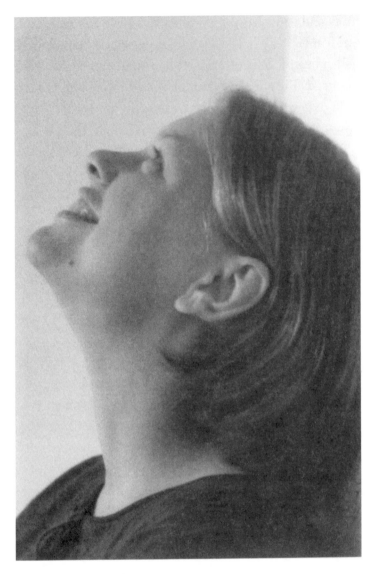

Nina, spring 1996

black and white close-up profiles that Nina had posed for. She leaned her head back and was gazing heavenward with a beatific look on her face and an unfamiliar hat on her head. The effect was stunning, as if I were looking at a girl I did not know. It gave me a new perspective of Nina and suffused the room with her being.

We slept in the basement of the Leighton's house. I was awake during the night, and when I fell back asleep I had a dream of Dennis and me holding Nina in our arms and saying goodbye to her as she died from an illness.

Eighth Holy Night
That night, another dream filled with color and light assured me that Nina's life and death were part of the creator's master plan, that all was well.

I had a few more notable dreams in January. In one of them I was in the funeral home with Nina's body, dressing her for the last time as I used to dress her as a little girl. Upon awakening, I felt the loss of all the moments of mothering my little girl and of that last act of mothering.

Capturing these dreams and feelings in my journal helped me remember and ponder them. They were a significant part of my healing journey. In my dreams, I said goodbye to Nina before she died and dressed her after she died, the two experiences that in reality, I missed. Equally significant, I got reassurance of Nina's spiritual wellbeing, and a glimpse of the exalted nature of her ongoing existence. I felt blessed by these visits from Nina.

I didn't dream about Nina or Kirsten until the next year

during the Holy Nights. Then out of the blue, a powerful dream came after sleeping soundly the whole night. It had a huge impact on me for many days.

December 30, 1997
Dennis and I were on the back of a pick-up truck with Nina's body, having reburied her in her coffin once or twice already. I had her in my arms. With her eyes closed, she said very quietly, "Mom." Of course, I couldn't believe my ears. When she said it again I got Dennis' attention. I hugged her as she woke up.

She told us that she had almost been ready to arise the last time we had re-buried her, but was upset when we left her again in terrible shape with sand in her eyes. I told her how Dennis regretted leaving her so quickly that time.

Nina got up and started striding away with a giant's pace. I followed her, trying hard to keep up with her and keep sight of her. It was summer, and she wore a light-weight, gauze gathered skirt, tank top, and bare feet. Other friends saw her as she walked through the fairgrounds to sit in the bleachers. I slipped in beside her, as did another friend. Then I woke up.

I was struck with how like her normal self Nina looked, with her limp hair hanging straight down; her bare feet tough and dirty. She did not seem radiant or angelic, but she was larger than life.

What was this dream about? What was I to do with it?

My first thought was that Nina was choosing to incarnate again on the earth already. But this did not

seem likely, given what I knew about the length of the
spiritual journey of the soul between death and rebirth.
As I have lived with this dream, I believe that it was a
reminder not to keep Nina tied to earth, but to allow her
the freedom of rebirth in the spirit.

Nina's dream visits to me ended with this dream.
This fills me with sadness. Dennis has frequent dreams
of Nina and I get jealous when he tells me about them.
He sleeps soundly every night and wakes almost every
morning remembering his dreams. I have more difficulty sleeping, often waking in the wee hours of the
morning, unable to fall back asleep, and only rarely
remember my dreams.

The difference in our constitution and sleep patterns
reflects the difference in the way we grieve. Dennis went
back to work sooner than I did, faithfully carrying out his
role as breadwinner. He allows himself very little self-
indulgence. However, his escape in sleep probably gives
him the renewal he needs to go on. His dreams give him
an ongoing connection to Nina.

Carrying On

Out of Seclusion

Six weeks after Nina's death, my time of seclusion came to an end. I resumed my normal routine of teaching at my parent-child playgroup (with Soren) on Tuesday and Friday mornings. On Thursday mornings I went to the Reading to the Dead group, then to the YWCA to go swimming.

Dennis and I also volunteered to direct singing for the twenty-five students at the Youth Initiative High School on Thursdays. We had been inspired by their singing at Nina's memorial service. They had no music director at the school and we felt we could fill this void. We had many songs living in us that we wanted to share, and this would be a good way to connect with the students, some of whom were friends with Nina and Kirsten, as well as with Kevin.

These activities on Thursdays were possible because Kim Pilgrim cared for Soren that day. The two remaining days I tended to regular household tasks with Soren by my side. I wrote in my journal when I was able. The following entries, spanning the time from January until Easter, show how I tried to cope with a roller coaster of emotions while carrying out routine responsibilities and new activities.

January 14, 1997
I put a huge effort of will into getting ready for my first playgroup today. I woke up early enough to get organized before Soren got up. The morning went beautifully and I loved being the teacher for these children. It was a good day—I felt strong until after supper. What a relief, I can do it again!

I feel more able to simplify now. I can clearly distinguish the essential from the non-essential, and care nothing about anything non-essential. In this mindset I am more able to hang loose and live in the moment. Perhaps I will be more efficient, as well.

January 27, 1997
I cried last night, not for missing Nina, but for being afraid of my life getting so full of responsibilities that the things that mean something to me personally will get crowded out. I still have a need to just sit and let things be and not always be directed. I still feel only able, at times, to tend to the basics. I try to give them my best and make them as lovely as possible (meals, especially). I need to have time to sing. Singing for me is letting a piece of heaven into my life in a more tangible way than just in thoughts. I need to write more. I would like to write poetry. I would like to write for Kevin and Soren.

February 2, 1997
On Thursday, the day Kim cares for Soren, I went for the second time to Mary Kay Hagon's house where she, Jennifer Fox, and I meet to read for Nina and Kirsten. Jennifer is on vacation now, but Linda is joining us. Today I felt such strength and gratitude for the worlds that are opening up before me. The ever-evolving nature of Christianity and its relationship to life after death, and the give and take between the worlds of life and death is so powerfully working upon me. At these times I can truly feel grateful to Nina and awed by the transformative nature of all that has happened.

From there I went on to swim and sauna, then to sing with the Youth Initiative. What a day!

The next morning, I woke up feeling somewhat empty, unable to feel Nina's presence. Why would this happen after all the richness of the day before?

Playgroup was hard on Friday. I felt tired of and unable to deal imaginatively with children running around the loop between rooms. In my plans, I felt inspired to tell a Candlemas nature story, but with only one helper, we ran too late and I didn't have the energy to pull it off.

Then, coming home to a cold, empty house on a gray day, I missed Nina so much that I cried and cried. I wanted to talk to someone in person, not on the phone. Soren and I went walking in the neighborhood, searching for someone at home. It was empty and cold – no shoulder to cry on. When we returned home I read Kirsten's journal (on loan from Linda) until Dennis came home. Then Dennis, Soren, and I met Kevin at a friend's house where we were invited for supper.

*Today, Sunday, Dennis made buttermilk pancakes
for breakfast. I got in a goofy mood with pent-up winter
energy and went dancing and running around the house.
Before long, the euphoria turned to tears and I ended up
in the shower weeping so hard I wanted to scream!!*

*Where is the place for silliness and laughter? Life at the
moment is so serious and somber! Kirsten in her journal
questioned where her dad's wildness and craziness went. I
question this too! Nina was never terribly silly around us,
but she and Kirsten together were totally silly. Kevin isn't
silly like them. Why did I have to lose all that silly girlish-
ness? Where do I go? What can I turn to? What can I do
with my life? Why am I the only one crying??*

February 14, 1997
  *I kneel at the open drawers of your dresser
  Like Mary at the empty tomb
  Weeping for my love, who is gone.
  All I am left with
  Are the empty folds of your clothing.
  Perhaps I shall fill them
  With my tears.*

  *Oh, soft, faded, frayed t-shirt—
  Caress my face!
  Rub all the years of her young, tender body-warmth
  Into the sad creases
  Etching themselves into my face,
  That they not be un-loved creases!
  Gladden my sorrow
  With the scent of her*

Which will not leave—
It is all I have left.

Yesterday I wanted to write a fairy tale
About your wondrous life.
Today I can only weep at the emptiness of today
And all the days to come.

March 18, 1997
I felt so strong yesterday going to Bill Van Stee's funeral
and reception, and then to the Compassionate Friends
meeting. There Dennis and I talked with a couple who
had lost their 18-month-old girl, Nina, to drowning only
three weeks ago. We felt drawn to them because our
daughters had the same name, but also because we rec-
ognized that state of early grief that they were in and felt
able to reach out to them from the perspective of being a
little further down the path.

I felt strong this morning and had the presentiment
that, following this strong period, I will soon be engulfed
by grief again. Knowing that it will come, what can I do to
ease the way—and do I want to be overwhelmed by it or
try to overcome it? After an extremely difficult morning in
preschool I felt the tendency to want to let down and let
the grief take over. I know that grief can be an escape from
the exhaustion of normal life.

I put forth my best effort in the morning but felt
that something else was at work amongst the children. I
needed to be there to help them bear it, no matter what,
and hold out against whatever forces were working
against harmony and love.

Then on the way home Samuel Barber's "Adagio for Strings" came from the car radio and threatened to make me crumble. Music is the most difficult thing for me to bear emotionally. It seems so close to the spiritual world. But there was something inside me saying, "You can hold out against this beauty, too; stand firm and know this is beautiful and must not make you sad." The music filled me with yearning.

I don't know what to yearn for. I don't know if it can come about on earth. Yet yearning for death is not the answer. Oh, life, what can I expect from you, when it seems that the most beautiful thing is death?

March 23, 1997
Because today was Palm Sunday, we made it a special Sunday. The most satisfying part was playing music with Dennis for a long time in the morning. Truly, it has been a long time since we have played saxophone and piano together. In the last few years I have played more with Nina and Kevin on their viola and cello.

Returning to pieces of music that we have played together for years brought unexpected joy. In that moment, I realized what a special connection Dennis and I have through playing music together. I found myself yearning to do it again. Perhaps music is what will make me feel beauty in life again.

March 30, 1997 (Easter Sunday)
My dearest Nina,
In the warm loving arms of everyone at Camphill, we have passed the anniversary of the fourth month after your

death. I was able to walk out alone and scan the rolling hills with the wind blowing hard, look down upon the sweetly winding river, see the sparkling, gurgling brook appear from under the snow, and hear the joyous song of spring birds returning in the soft, friendly woods. You live so vibrantly in all of these places. It was a comfort to my soul to be here, loving you.

New Reality

The time between Christmas and Easter were months of adjustment to living with a new reality. I still felt like I was in a dream, for I walked through the normal events of a day largely unaware of my loss. When the thought, "My daughter has died," reappeared, my world turned topsy-turvy. All of a sudden, nothing seemed normal, and I was clutching my heart and sobbing, alone with the all consuming pain of loss, wondering how I could go on living. This violent emotion would work its way out and leave me exhausted, my face aching the rest of the day. A new day could bring fresh energy, or when I woke the morning after intense grieving, I might feel flat and wrung out.

Many activities, when experienced for the first few times after Nina's death, had associations that were excruciatingly painful. One of them was going to the Linden Hills Co-op, where I regularly shopped for groceries, since we had no co-op near our home. I hadn't gotten back into the routine of making the special trip to Linden Hills, about ten miles from home. The Berghs lived right around the corner from the co-op. Nina spent many hours with Kirsten, and I knew that they often popped over to the co-op for a smoothie or some other necessity.

The first time I went to the co-op, I could only see Nina and Kirsten. I wanted to say to everyone there, "Don't you remember Nina—she used to come here all the time, and now she's gone forever." I didn't know anyone there personally, so I couldn't say anything. I couldn't keep myself from crying as I walked through the aisles, trying to accomplish my task. Then I stopped the tears and put on a smile at the check-out counter as if everything was fine. This became a familiar pattern.

On the days that I went to my twice a week parent-child playgroup in southwest Minneapolis, I drove Kevin to his school. We often turned on the radio or a tape player to pass the time on the long drive. Whatever kind of music we listened to had some sort of association with Nina for me. It inevitably led to tears. I sensed that Kevin was in agony at these times, putting up with so much crying, though he didn't say anything.

I almost always cried while driving, when I was forced to be still. I wondered why I never noticed other people crying in their cars. Surely there were many reasons for people to cry—why did I never see anyone else succumbing to tears as they drove?

I cried a lot on the weekends, too, as I did when Nina first left home for New York. When we were all together, I was painfully aware of the gaps where one more should have been—the fifth place at the table, the fifth napkin ring, the cubby with her name still on it above a coat hook in the basement. Whatever the activity, I was reminded of this great loss we were enduring. When I was dusting, for example, and came to her sculptures, I stroked them in desperate longing to somehow "touch" her being in the clay she had sculpted with her hands.

Many nights I slept in Nina's bed, burying my nose in her favorite holey t-shirt, letting it absorb my tears.

Every now and then, I declined to participate in a family activity away from home, claiming some time to be alone in the house. Then I could wail all I wanted with no thought to what affect it might be having on someone else. This was my time to be with Nina, to listen to the music that brought her presence so near, to read her journal or letters or school essays, or write in my own journal. I always found something which connected me to her essence. I came out of these times feeling close to her and inspired to do something, be it to write a letter or call a certain person, or play a certain piece of music or song for some occasion. These times were crucial for my recovery.

Life Review and Reading

The focus of my energy during the time between Christmas and Easter, beyond maintaining necessary activities, was twofold. One focus was to lovingly record all of the events just before or around Nina's death with what she had left for us and what the world gave to us. This included a scrapbook and two photo albums.

I had given Nina a scrapbook when she left for Harlemville, but she had not put anything in it. I gathered the goodbye and birthday cards that were left in the pile on Nina's desk, school notices about her activities, the monthly school calendar with the "My Mom is coming!" note on November 6, newspaper articles covering the accident, her unsent letters, notices of her death from various publications, and poems written by friends. I mourned over each of these items before I mounted them in the scrapbook.

Annamaria had given Nina a blank book for recording her life in pictures when they parted from Camphill. Nina had gathered photos of herself and her friends from her childhood and youth as well as some pictures of Oma (Nina's grandma) from various stages of her life to put in this book. I finished what Nina had started, writing captions to identify each photo that I mounted. I also filled another album with photos of Nina that had not previously been put in an album, starting with the last photo I had taken of her meeting Uncle Alan on Fern Hill in New York, documenting her life in reverse order.

It took several months to complete these books. Every picture was lovingly gazed at and cried over. Sharing these three books with friends and family gave me a way to talk about the whole experience of Nina's life and death, my entire world at the time.

While working on scrapbooks and photo albums, I had another focus— reading about death. Dennis and I were given several books which helped us immensely. We started to read one while in Harlemville. *Where Are You?* was written by Karin v. Schilling, a mother from a Camphill Village in South Africa, who had also lost a child in a car accident. It helped me to hear how another mother nurtured her relationship to her deceased child.

Its practical suggestions made it invaluable, and I kept it close to me for a long time.

The second book, *Citizens of the Cosmos: Life's Unfolding from Conception Through Death to Rebirth,* by Beredene Jocelyn, was also invaluable. I read certain sections of the second part, "Our Journey Through the Cosmos Between Death and Rebirth," over and over again. It was comforting to have some idea of what Nina's journey looked like. As much as I admit to being a student of Anthroposophy, there were gaping holes in my basic reading and understanding. I had not read the sections on life after death that are included in many of Steiner's basic books. Now that I needed this information, I drank it in ravenously, and was grateful to have access to this great spiritual bounty.

The third book that I found helpful was *Life Beyond Death, Selected Lectures,* by Rudolf Steiner. This book was more challenging to read, but persistence yielded great pearls of wisdom. These lectures about the relationship between the living and the "so-called dead" led me to initiate a group to read for the those who have died. This group started to meet in January.

At first, meeting with a small group of friends gave me a way to have regular support in making sense of Nina's death. Reading to Nina and Kirsten gave us a focus. Steiner postulates that those who have died receive the spiritual thoughts of human beings as nourishment. Knowing that I could help them where they were now, I grasped onto reading to Nina and Kirsten as something I could do for them on a regular basis. Thursday morning was one time out of my busy week that I devoted entirely to them.

I was grateful to have two friends to begin doing this
with me. Mary Kay Hagan and Jennifer Fox had recently
lost their mothers, so were also interested in this work.
Within four or five weeks, Linda had recuperated enough
to join us. Dennis wanted to be a part of this activity
as well. He arranged his work so that he could take off
Thursday morning most weeks. Other people joined the
group for shorter or longer periods, but this core group of
five would continue over the next three years.

I had a sense that reading to the dead was part of our
task in the community. We were pioneers in awakening
people to the reality of life after death, to the presence
of our deceased loved ones in our lives, and in nurturing a relationship with them. We sought to transform
the tragedy of Nina and Kirsten's deaths into a purpose-
ful and meaningful event for our whole community.
Because Dennis, Linda, and I were intimately linked to
this tragedy, we were the ones to begin cultivating this
relationship with those across the threshold, with the
help of our two friends who also felt this to be a part of
their mission.

Where Two or Three are Gathered

We began our Reading for the Dead gatherings by
pouring tea and lighting a candle. Then one person
read a verse for the dead. In a period of silence, we each
inwardly named those we knew who had crossed the
threshold and invited them to join us in our reading.

At our first gathering I intuitively chose a verse by
Rudolf Steiner, which we continued to use thereafter. It

evokes an intimacy with the dead by calling upon our
personal love to be transformed to soul love and directed
to spirit light. It further unites us with the dead by placing
us beside them in their mode of being, experiencing with
them their interest in the world.

May love of hearts reach out to love of souls,
May warmth of love ray out to Spirit-light.
Even so would we draw near to you,
Thinking with you Thoughts of Spirit,
Feeling with you the Love of Worlds,
Consciously at one with you,
Willing in silent Being.

Many times during those first months at these gatherings I felt Nina's presence so closely that I could hardly
bear the pain and beauty of it. At these times it was only
with great effort of will that I was able to concentrate
on our reading. There were several times when I did not
accomplish this and could only sit and listen and cry.
What kept me coming back to the group was the power
of gathering "two or three together" to break through
the barriers between the world of the living and the
world of the dead.

We began reading aloud passing the book around
every few pages, and allowing ourselves the freedom to
express questions or comments to help illuminate the
text. Other Reading for the Dead groups that we had
heard about did not include conversation in their read-
ings. We felt that the conversations that arose enlivened
our group, and thus we hoped enlivened the thoughts
perceived by the circle of souls to whom we were

reading. We closed by reading the verse once again, having a period of silence, and extinguishing the candle.

We first began to read Nina's confirmation lessons from Christian Community priest Greg Brewer, which I had stored away so long ago. Personally, these held meaning for me because I had shared them with Nina when she was 14, and was now sharing them with her again. The group found that the six lessons about the healings in the Gospel of St. John had the depth and tone that was perfect for getting us started while we discussed what major book we wanted to read.

Our first impulse was to read something from the Waldorf high school curriculum that Nina and Kirsten had missed. After considering other books by Steiner, we decided that something relevant to their lives would also be the most meaningful to us. Besides, most of us had not read or studied these works ourselves!

We chose *The Speech of the Grail* by Linda Sussman, a book about Parzival, a 12th century epic read in the eleventh grade in some Waldorf schools. It includes a retelling of the Parzival story and its relevance for the modern person. We were so intrigued by it that we went on to read the original *Parzival* by Wolfram von Eschenbach, published in 1477.

Parzival is a timeless story of the journey of a young man, raised in complete protection from the outer world, who as a youth, goes out into the world and has many rude awakenings. The winding road he takes to find his destiny can be an affirmation for students at the age when they are seeking their own destiny, but encountering failures and confusion along the way. There are implications for all of us, young and old, on a path of self-discovery. I continually found ways to relate Parzival's story to Nina's life, and to my own.

We went on to read *Faust*, the play by German poet Johann Wolfgang von Goethe, which is studied in the 12th grade of the Waldorf high school. These three books took us through the first year.

Our group, all parents of high school students, accompanied the formative years of the Waldorf high school in the Twin Cities (starting with grades 9 and 10 in 1996). Through reading what the high school students would be reading in the coming years, we felt that we were helping prepare the ground for them, and thus supporting the commitment to Waldorf education that was so important to Nina and Kirsten.

Two of Us

The winter months were a time of discovery. Dennis and I were still finding out new things about Nina's life. Friends sent us long-lost photos we hadn't seen before. Others whom we hadn't known before wrote and shared their memories with us. These were both heartwarming and heart wrenching.

The Hawthorne Valley School dedicated their winter edition of the school newspaper, Valley View, to poems, stories, and other tributes written by students and faculty in memory of Nina and Kirsten. The Armstrong Odyssey, from Nina's public high school, also printed a memorial article about Nina. The volume of tributes to Nina caused me to wonder at the impact one life can have.

I made the most amazing discovery one Sunday morning in February. I had brought home the postcards and note cards that Nina had displayed in her room in Harlemville and remounted them in her room in our home. I walked into her room and saw that one of the cards from her collection had fallen onto the floor. I picked it up and found a note card with a message written inside to Nina from Kirsten. It was dated November 28, 1996, the day before they died. I couldn't believe what I was reading. I couldn't figure out how or why this could have been written when it was.

I showed the card to Dennis, who was equally perplexed and amazed. Then I called Linda. I described the photo on the front of the card of two little girls wearing only underwear and rubber boots and holding hands as they walked in the mud. Linda recognized it right away as a card that Kirsten had bought in Minneapolis in August for Nina's October birthday. Evidently, Kirsten hadn't given it to her on her birthday. Kirsten must have found the card when she cleaned her room before leaving to pick her mother up from the airport and written these words:

Nov. 28, 1996
To Nina, my love,
Listening to "Two of Us" (Beatles), joy fills me, shimmers through me, knowing that although we've made so many thousands of sunny or cloudy memories together, "the road that stretches out ahead" will be so much longer—so many adventures and loves and laughter and tears and sorrow—just so much life lies before us, the "two of

us." How we will grow strong and beautiful (even more than we are now!) and become grannies together—rosy, apple-cheeked, cloudy-haired grandmothers who will tell stories to the grandbabies about iced-grapefruit chapstick and moose and about our childhood loves and losses, about the hours and days spent together, the years, the centuries; two girls becoming women.

And then we'll cackle at each other with twinkling eyes and laugh till we cry, and then when they all go to sleep, or go away, we'll slip on our Converse and go dancing the night away under the moonlight. But that is many years, many miles away. Our feet will dance over so much earth, our ears hear so much music, our hands touch so many people, our hearts love so much! And I'll see you golden and glowing with babies and me too perhaps. And the world will be a little bit better because of us, even if our names are forgotten after our death. But death won't stop us, it's only another lake to swim, another slight climb before the next mountain peak.

But 'till then, 'till tomorrow, I'll remember to love the snow, and you'll begin to love skirts over Sorrells and the world and life will hold us like a mother. Happy life, dear sister.

Kirsten

The last sentence of Kirsten's letter swings between the detailed familiarity of the everyday world and the vision of being cradled by the cosmic mother. The ending wish for a happy life conveys absolute trust in what the universe might hold for these soul mates.

Kirsten's dream of the two of them growing old

together could lead people to mourn the tragedy of their dying so young. I felt this tragic reality. My heart broke when I read Kirsten's letter.

Ultimately, however, it had the opposite effect, prompting me to appreciate the wonder that two young women could feel so connected with the universe and their destiny. Moving between the microcosmic and macrocosmic, Kirsten acknowledged to Nina the strong karmic bond between them that would take them through death together. Her letter became the silver thread tying together the pieces of the luminous story of Nina and Kirsten's lives.

Spring

✣

She Would Draw Flowers

Linda held a memorial service for Kirsten the week after Easter. She had gone home from the hospital after six weeks, when her mouth was no longer wired shut, and she could begin to eat normal food. She had slowly regained strength as she recuperated at home, until she could get out of bed, get dressed, and prepare simple meals for herself. In her recovery she had fallen and broken a toe and was wearing a cast. She was not free of crutches as she had hoped when the time for the memorial came around, but at least she could sustain limited times of activity.

Many of the people now so important in our lives were coming from New York to attend. Bruce and Karen Frishkoff stayed at our house. The Elinson family and a few other students from Harlemville stayed at the Bergh/O'Brien household. Dennis' parents and some of Linda's friends from California also traveled to Minnesota for this event.

At the time, we three were engaged in reliving and assimilating the accident, the wake and funeral, and Nina and Kirsten's life in Harlemville. We found it helpful to connect with the people who were impacted by it. Many of the crucial figures in the last chapter of their lives gathered together, telling the story again.

The night before the memorial service, Linda had a gathering at her house. She gave a copy of *She Would Draw Flowers* to each of us.

Linda, amazingly, had put together this book of Kirsten's poetry and artwork during her recovery. Just as I had poured over Nina's pictures, letters, and other memorabilia and made scrapbooks, Linda poured over Kirsten's sketchbooks and journals and published a book. Kirsten, a prolific writer as well as a gifted artist, had written in a journal every day for years, and kept an idea book with her at all times.

I recall the moment in Linda's living room when I opened *She Would Draw Flowers.* First I saw and read Kirsten's letter to Nina of November 28 on the opening page. Then I came upon the photo I had taken seven months earlier of Nina and Kirsten at the airport as they departed for Harlemville. Their heads are touching, Nina's hand rests on Kirsten's shoulder, and they are beaming. On the page with this photo is Kirsten's poem, "For Nina and Me." Linda had shown me this sweet poem before, with its allusions to our backpacking trip in Montana, such as the naming of flavors for the lip balms we used on our wind-dried lips. Seeing it in print with the photo of the two of them on the day we said goodbye to them was stunning. It was like the moment before Nina's memorial, when I was totally taken aback and couldn't believe they were gone. I could have wept again in desperation, but the presence of others prevented me from giving full rein to my emotions. However, as I looked around at others in the silent room, I noticed others' eyes welling up. Dennis and I leaned into each other for support.

Our community came out in full force to support Linda and honor Kirsten. Many of the people who had attended Nina's memorial in December attended Kirsten's in April. Linda held the service at the Lake Harriet Church where Paul's and Nina's memorials had both been. Barbara McAfee had gathered people to play in a band, including Dennis on the saxophone and Patrick O'Brien on the accordion. Their rendition of "How Can I Keep from Singing" was a highlight. Zusha and other students from New York also played music, including our beloved "Ashokan Farewell."

Cecelia retold the story of the accident. As I visualized Nina and Kirsten's deaths, I imagined the moment when their spirits were freed from confinement in a body, and sent this thought to them. This brought me peace.

At the end of the service, Linda passed out copies of *She Would Draw Flowers* to all who were there. After the service, people adjourned to the fellowship hall in the basement for food and dancing. The crying and mourning during the service were breathed out in laughter and fun.

Caretaking

A few days after Kirsten's memorial, Soren and I rode with Dennis' parents as they drove back to Fort Wayne, Indiana. It was a relief to be with Soren in the back seat on the 12-hour drive with Grandpa and Grandma, and in their home, with someone else being "in charge." I didn't have to drive, figure out where we were going, or make any decisions. I was free to just enjoy playing with almost five-year-old Soren, a rarity in the busyness of everyday life. We read books, recited little verses with finger motions, drew pictures, made up stories with finger puppets, and played cards. We spent one night in a motel where I slept in a room with Soren. I wrote in my journal, "I need not be lonely, for my Nina is with me."

After a night in Fort Wayne, Soren and I drove my father-in-law's car to Bloomington, Indiana, to stay with my mother for five days while my stepfather visited his daughter in Alaska. Now I was in charge again, and had the terrifying experience of falling asleep at the wheel for a half second. This sent me into a tizzy, for I had no one to take over for me. I had to figure out how to cope alone.

When Soren and I got to my mother and Wayne's apartment in the Meadowood Retirement Center, I was overcome with sadness with all the "what-ifs" in my life that being in my mother's home brought up. What if my dad had not died when he was 48? What if my mother hadn't gotten Parkinson's? What if Nina were still living?

Here in my mother's home, which used to be a refuge for me, where I could always depend on "being taken care of," the tables were turned. I had to be in charge, taking care of my mother. In her Alzheimer's/Parkinson's daze, Mom's emotional life appeared to have been left behind somewhere, and now I had to leave my emotions behind also. I felt like I was parenting another preschooler. I needed to tie her shoes and zip her jacket before we went out. I had to put her to bed. I had to be aware of her as I slept, should she get up in the night.

At this stage in her illness, Mom still tried to carry on conversations, but could not express herself completely or carry thoughts through to the end. I knew that she had taken in the fact of Nina's death, for she mentioned hearing about the accident at Thanksgiving several times. She had chosen a lovely photo of Nina at age 14 to have enlarged and put in a gold frame. Yet she never engaged me in a conversation about Nina, as she would have two years earlier. I imagine that, if she were able, she would have been present emotionally for me at Nina's death just as she had been present at the time of Nina's birth. I longed for that so much.

There was, however, a wonderful aspect to this visit. Soren and my mom seemed to be on the same wavelength. When we went for walks outside, Soren found a walking stick like my mom's and was the "old man." My mom laughed about Soren imitating her and at the picture the two of them made walking along together, or perhaps it was just at the joy of walking along with him. We have a few photos that capture the beauty of their relationship at this last "coherent" visit.

My coping abilities were being stretched to the max during our five-day stay at Meadowood.

When my stepfather returned, I took a long hike

outside amidst the redbud and dogwood trees blooming in the woods on the Meadowood campus. This helped me endure the last day there. Wayne's inimitable energy and enthusiasm buoyed us all, but I was ready to go home.

Soren and I drove the car back to Fort Wayne, and Dennis' parents drove us to Chicago to catch the train home to Minnesota.

New Layers

April turned to May, and spring arrived in Minnesota. With a new season came new layers of grief. I asked myself many times if I would have done anything different had I known that our time with Nina would be so short. I wondered why so many things seemed important, when in the end they didn't matter at all. For example, I remembered how Dennis and I struggled to get her to learn word processing keyboarding correctly, since she would be using the computer in high school and college, and her whole life. She hadn't learned to type as part of her Waldorf education, so we bought her a program to learn it on her own. The Mavis Beacon program was a series of lessons that required regular practice sessions. We had to remind and prod her repeatedly, and Nina did not go down the basement stairs to the computer with joy in her step. In the end, what did it matter if she only typed 20 words per minute with the hunt and peck method?

What did it matter if Nina learned a foreign language, or got a job, or had a high grade point average? What did it matter if she watched television or not, or knew how to make a white sauce, knit socks, or print in calligraphy? Our personal and societal values came into question, when life itself seemed so fragile.

This journal entry expressed this dilemma and my conclusion.

May 3, 1997
> *Senseless it is*
> *To have raised a child*
> *Only to have her*
> *Taken from us*
> *Before the task*
> *Had its fulfillment.*
>
> *Wisdom it was*
> *That we did not know the master plan,*
> *For how could we have raised a child*
> *Knowing how the task*
> *Would be fulfilled?*

We raised her as best we could, for she was ours to love and nurture, regardless of the outcome.

May Day

Dennis, Soren, and I went to the Minneapolis Powderhorn Park May Day festival that spring. We hadn't attended in recent years, but Nina and Kirsten had gone the previous year, which became our reason for going again. Although it had been cold for them the previous May, it was perfect weather this year. We sat on the grassy hill watching the Heart of the Beast Theater's annual enactment of the return of the sun from across the lake, complete with larger than life puppets and a man on stilts. As the throngs of people passed by, I was continuously searching for girls like Nina, imagining her doing the same kinds of things they were doing at this popular community gathering.

Then I saw a young man, tall and well-built, with long, straight dark hair and a gentle look. I imagined that Nina would have liked him. All of a sudden I saw Nina leaning into his chest, totally comfortable and in love. The image was so real I felt confused. At the same time, in a strange way, I felt at peace, seeing in such a vivid way what might have been for Nina. It gave me assurance that she would have been loved, just as she was, by a gorgeous human being. It brought on a great melancholy as well, grieving for all the things that might have been.

Dennis said on the way home that, had Nina lived, we might have been grandparents within five years. This was entirely possible given Nina's motherly inclinations. But now, there was little possibility of being grandparents for a long time. Kevin, we imagined, would take years to start a family. It probably would be two decades into the future before Soren would even approach this stage of life. We weren't longing to become grandparents, but the realization of our loss in such specific terms saddened us.

I had kept a box of wooden rattles, hand-knit silk hats and wool sweaters labeled "Baby Things for Nina" in storage, knowing that my daughter would cherish these items. Now they would not be appreciated in the same way. They could never hold the same tenderness for our sons or for a daughter-in-law. I will keep this box, with its label, and move it with me wherever I go, cherishing the thought, never to be realized, of Nina with her first-born baby.

Nina's Story

With my scrapbooks and photo albums completed, I had the inspiration to write the story of Nina's life in the form of a fairy tale. The idea had been forming for a few months; I only needed the time, clarity of mind, and some coaching to write it. I accomplished my goal over three weeks, with the help of Christina Beck, so that I had it ready to read at a ceremony to spread Nina's ashes.

We had been waiting until the ground thawed to do something with Nina's ashes. We were also waiting until Gwyneth and Annamaria were both in Minnesota. Our friends at Camphill Village Minnesota lovingly embraced our wishes to scatter the ashes in a place where Nina could be remembered in the Village. Gwyneth and Annamaria helped to choose a spot in a woodland area near a little creek. They cleared and mowed it so that some plantings could be made in Nina's honor, and called it the Sacred Garden.

We set the first weekend of June for our ceremony. We arrived the night before to prepare. We didn't have an urn for Nina's ashes; they were still in the round tin can inside a sturdy cardboard box. Debbie Leighton provided a tall and narrow ceramic bowl to ceremoniously hold the ashes during the service. We enlisted the help of several people to carry out different parts of the ceremony.

We gathered the next morning in the hall of the Kaethe Meinicke Building, the same room where our three children were christened, where we had played and sung music, had parties, listened to lectures, and celebrated festivals over the five years we had lived at Camphill. Almost all of the people in the Village, as well as friends from outside the Village, came for this gathering. Nina's group of Camphill friends was there: Gwyneth, Annamaria, Nic, Ciaran, and, of course, Kevin. Those forty people made it a true community event.

Dennis read some words by Rudolf Steiner about the importance of human remains enlivening the earth. Then we all walked in a procession, singing, down the hill to the little bridge over the creek. Here we sang a song Nina had taught to our family: "The River is flowing, flowing and growing, the river is flowing, down to the sea. Mother carry me, child I will always be; Mother carry me, home to the sea. Spirit of the wind, carry me home to my Self." Dennis, carrying the bowl of ashes, threw some of them into the creek where they would flow into the Sauk River, then into the Mississippi River, and down to the sea. This was a most tender moment, bringing Dennis to tears, making it difficult for him, and the rest of us, to sing.

Then we proceeded to the Sacred Garden in the woods.

We approached the Garden from a path through tall meadow grasses. When we stepped over a big fallen tree, we were in a mowed area that forms the southern loop of the space prepared for this memorial garden. Here, Gwyneth and Annamaria had created a campfire ring with logs and stones for sitting on, inspired by

the many campfires and sleep-outs that Nina and her
friends had enjoyed at Camphill.

Then, the path goes through a narrow crossing point
between some shrubs into the northern loop. This area is
mostly shaded, so the grass is thin and interspersed with
weeds, saplings, and a few newly planted wildflowers
along the edge of the woods. Another Camphill couple,
who had a stillborn baby boy, planted two mountain ash
trees, with two wind chimes hanging from their branches,
and flowering bulbs in his memory in a ring at the northern edge of this area of the garden. The grounds crew of
the Village made some lovely log benches to add to the
natural setting.

We all made a large circle encompassing the whole
northern loop. Nancy Potter began this portion of the
ceremony by reading the story of Nina's life that I had
written. I was eager to share this story which portrayed
the richness, beauty, and meaning of Nina's life in images.

NINA'S STORY
Once there lived a young man and a young woman who,
having been raised by good and pious parents in differ-
ent cities, ventured away from home, with their parents'
blessings, to seek their destiny. Being both of sensible and
inquisitive natures, they first sought the council of wise
men and women at a center of higher learning. They
each found themselves pursuing the secrets of life and
love from the most sublime of teachers, music, and thus
occupied, they chanced to meet. When they played music
together, their very souls resonated with a song of long life
in close harmony.

And so they went forth into the wide world together. Many an adventure they had as they traveled the world o'er, and before long a sweet melody called them back to the land of their birth. There they celebrated their wedding. Soon came the voice of their first-born child, whispering in love, "I am coming, mother, but first you must learn how to receive me." Again they set off into the world. They trudged through ice and snow and climbed high mountains until they caught a glimpse of their very own stars shining forth from the dome of heaven, illuminating a path of knowledge for them. This assurance guided their steps to a home where they could welcome their children into earthly life.

One autumn night, when the frost came and bid farewell to the last leaves of summer on the trees, a baby girl was born to the man and woman. In their hearts they heard the song of her name, Nina Christine. Wherever they walked, the birds, the flowers, the trees, the sylphs, and undines, all of creation bowed down before them.

The baby grew into a wee little girl with soft blond hair and blue eyes, and was a joy to her parents. They had too much love for three, and then they became four. A baby boy, Kevin Andreas, was born to the man and woman. The little family grew and struggled and basked in the surrounding love of grandparents, aunts and uncles, and new little cousins.

Soon came the call again to adventure away, this time to the far northland. In this new place, the shy little girl, Nina, went to school and watched her schoolmates. She loved them all, but was especially glad when her family became friends with Kirsten and her parents, Paul and Linda. They spent many an hour hiking or skiing and talking together.

At this same time, a young woman named Laura began to visit Nina's family and shy little Nina heard a voice in her ear whispering, "This is someone who you can trust and love. Do not be afraid." So they became friends, and then Laura became her godmother.

When Nina was just starting to turn into a big girl, her family took a trip to the country and visited a farm where a lot of people lived together in a most unusual fellowship. Nina's angel whispered to her bewildered parents, "This is where you need to be." So they packed up once again and joined this community. Such beautiful meadows, woodlands, streams, and rivers there were to play in and around, and two girls, Gwyneth and Annamaria, to play with! Nina played and played until she was ready to put her play things away. Then one of Nina's dearest wishes was granted and Nina was overjoyed: a new baby, Soren Peter, joined the family. This was cause for a grand celebration; not only Soren, but Nina and Kevin also were christened. Paul joined Laura as Nina's godfather. Close on the heels of the christening came Nina's confirmation. Now all was in place.

With her two dear friends, Nina began to prepare for her wedding far in the future. The three girls learned to cook and bake, spin and knit, clean and sew, draw and paint, grow flowers and herbs, dance and sing, canoe and hike—all that a young woman needs to know. When they were ready, they sang for all the community in sweet purity of the wedding that was awaiting them. Soon thereafter, the three maidens parted, each going off to seek their love.

Out in the wide, wide world, Nina found that all was not as she had dreamed. At first she felt lost amidst the throngs of strangers, the maze of hard streets, the drone of city noise. But the song of her wedding kept singing in her heart, and she gathered flowers to wear in her hair, so that her love might find her in the crowds. The fragrance of the flowers lured many to her who longed for a waft of the heavenly sweetness. There was one familiar face amidst the new ones who also wore flowers in her hair. Magnetically, they were drawn together again and again. This was none other than her girlhood friend, Kirsten. As they skipped and frolicked together with maidenly glee, the death of Paul came to try and daunt them. But the pain and sorrow they bore together, and lived their dreams all the more fervently.

No longer could the life within the cocoon of their families hold them. They must burst forth and fly away to a land awaiting them far from their homes. But so many obstacles stood in their path of flight. At the right moment, Laura was there as the beacon—pointing the way and preparing the ground so that all was made ready for them to arrive. Before Nina left, she chose new clothing appropriate for her new life, and, with her mother's help, prepared the white dress intended for her wedding. In the splendor of their newly fashioned garments, Nina and Kirsten left home with their parents' blessings.

With hearts full of hope, they tenderly approached their new surroundings and entered into their new life.

Very quickly they found others wearing flowers in their hair, but the flowers were all different from theirs. Just as Nina and Kirsten delighted in the new colors, forms, and fragrances, so did those they met delight in their flowers and the newness that they brought. And so, they all began to exchange flowers and weave new flower crowns together.

As Nina wove her new crown, the radiance of its beauty caused her heart to sing in ecstatic remembrance the song of her wedding. Every night the angels spoke more and more clearly to her so that she woke up one morning and said to herself, "You have found your love." Quietly and lovingly she unpacked the white wedding dress and hung it up to wait for the destined hour. She took Kirsten by the hand and they ran with light footsteps up hills and mountains to the pinnacle where earth met heaven. They then sang out, for all the world to hear, the joyous strains of the angels on high:

"GLORIA IN EXCELSIS DEO"

The story ended with everyone singing "Angels We Have Heard on High," the Christmas carol with the endless "glorias" that Nina and Kirsten were known to burst into at any time of the year. No one could sing it with the gusto that is the mood of the song at Christmas time, yet participants did sing with reverence for Nina and Kirsten and the joy with which they lived their lives. Looking around that circle through my tears, I saw many other teary faces.

The time came to plant the flowering crab tree and lilac bushes that Gwyneth and Annamaria chose for

Nina's memorial garden. Community members had already dug the holes, and now all were invited to take a handful of Nina's ashes to put in the holes or anywhere else in the garden. I was moved to see everyone—four-year-old child, forty-year-old parent, deaf man, teenager, and differently-abled residents Evelyn, Danny, Paul, (and many others)—reverently take the ashes from the bowl Dennis held and scatter them in a special place. Each of these individuals had been a part of our lives and some had lived with us when our children were growing up. Each had idiosyncrasies, both endearing and annoying. With varying levels of understanding, all were here to pay respect to a friend who had moved on to another realm. Their participation perfectly reflected Nina's inclusive spirit.

As we planted the trees and shrubs, Debbie read a poem Dennis and I had chosen for this occasion. Its beautiful image of letting go of the physical form of the body "like a petal back to the earth," reflected for all the ritual we had just completed. Having it read helped everyone depart in peace. It completed Nina's story.

Dennis and I saved some of Nina's ashes for scattering in other places and for the pottery urn that a friend was making for us. We were glad we had waited to have this ceremony at Camphill and that we had this beautiful place to remember our daughter. The experience of creating a sacred space together united the community in love and filled our hearts for a long time.

Summer

*

Pilgrimage

A week later, right after school was out for summer
vacation, Dennis and I took Kevin and Soren back to
New York for the graduation of Nina's high school
class. Dennis and I longed to be in Harlemville, where
our dear one still lived in the hearts of so many people.
Linda had been there a week earlier so she could connect with students while they were still in school, and
she was still there the first two days of our visit.

We would have traveled to this rite of passage, had
our daughter lived. We invited our relatives, as we
would have, had she lived. My brother Alan and his family came from Vermont and spent several days in Harlemville with us.

This graduation was charged with more emotion than
it would have had under normal circumstances. It forever changed our family's attitude toward these rites of
passage. We could never again take them for granted.

We unfortunately missed the first event surrounding
the actual graduation ceremony, the performance of the

senior class musical, *Fiddler on the Roof*. Nina had been
looking forward to acting and singing in this play for
which she had been student director at Armstrong High
School in Minnesota. It was a strange coincidence that
Hawthorne Valley School in New York had chosen the
same musical. The class dedicated their performance,
"To the memory of Nina Dietzel."

On the morning of the last day of school, we participated in the rose ceremony. This ritual mirrored one
from the first day of school, when the twelfth graders had
presented each of the first graders with a rose. Now the
first graders presented each of the seniors with a rose.
Since Nina was not there to receive her red rose, a little
girl presented it to me. All were touched by this gesture.
Dennis, Kevin, and I offered music to show our appreciation to the school community. We added the exuberance
of a Vivaldi sonata on piano, saxophone, and cello to this
solemn ceremony.

There was an exhibit of students' work on display
for the weekend. I wondered what Nina's main lesson
books would have looked like. I read other students'
books and cried at her having missed certain main
lesson subjects that she would have especially enjoyed.
I wondered how she would have accomplished and
presented her senior project, which had been to write
a play. I talked to some of her classmates. I saw the boy
that Nina had a crush on and wondered if her hoped-
for romance would have blossomed.

On Saturday night the seniors were all dressed up
for the graduation ceremony. I wondered if Nina would
have worn fancy shoes like most of the girls, or just her

favorite Birkenstocks. I wondered if Kirsten would have helped her shop for shoes and a dress. The commencement speaker reflected on the impact the death of Nina and Kirsten had on this class. The valedictorian spoke of a moment on the beach under a starlit sky when the students felt Nina's presence during their class trip to the Bahamas. The list of graduates in the program concluded with the words, "In loving memory of Nina Dietzel."

The high school choir sang several songs during the ceremony. The one that left the strongest impression was an Icelandic folk song in minor mode called "The Elk Herd."

Evening finds the elk herds departing
From the dunes and lakeside sands.
And the night, the all-embracing mother
Spreads her mantle o'er the silent land.

Bowing low, they drink the crystal water,
Stars reflecting like the heav'ns above,
Raise their heads and through their mighty antlers,
Summer winds sweep gently as a dove.

Silently, they leave the misty shores then,
Remnants of a long-forgotten day.
And they vanish in the distant spaces,
Through the portal of eternity.

This song, with its mournful melody, moving harmonies, and powerful images, captured the tone of the year for all of us: in silence and awe, in the night of existence, we stood together at the "portal of eternity" and got a glimpse of its profundity.

Journey into Nina's Space

We had brought some of Nina's ashes with us to Harlemville. Linda had brought some of Kirsten's ashes as well. The day after we arrived, there was a ceremony to plant a willow tree in honor of Nina and Kirsten near the creek on the Hawthorne Valley school grounds. Linda stayed long enough to be a part of this ceremony. A small group, including my brother and his family, the Elinsons, the Frishkoffs, and the Summers, gathered to join us in spreading Nina and Kirsten's ashes under that willow tree. Here we were again with this group of people who had become so close, gathered in the place where they all found themselves connected to our two girls at the beginning of the school year that had just ended. We shed tears at the poignancy of this destiny for all of us.

We spent one afternoon with Alan, Andrea, and their children, Rylan, Amelia, and Nevan, playing by the creek. That evening our two families went to the accident site on Route 217 three miles out of Harlemville. Where the highway curves to the right and comes to a rise, you can see the Catskill Mountains in the distance to the southwest. Five yards from the shoulder at the crest, on the north side of the highway, were remnants of spring flowering bulbs that the students had planted and stones they had placed there to mark the site. Nina's friend Daniel from Camphill Village Minnesota, who now lived near Harlemville, had made a wooden cross and set it upright in the ground beside the stones.

We sat on blankets while the sun set, singing camp songs, reading "Nina's Story," and spreading more of Nina's cremains. Holding Nina's ashes and returning them to the earth gave completion to my brother, sister-in-law, niece and nephews' experience of the wake and funeral six months before. We felt deeply connected as we shared this beautiful ritual together.

The day after the graduation ceremony, my brother's family left. We had one more place to spread some ashes. The next day our family walked with Cecelia, Sarah, and Zusha to one of the teenagers' favorite spots in the woods on the Elinson property. Linda had been there a few days before, and buried some of Kirsten's ashes and created a stone memorial. We buried the remaining few handfuls of Nina's ashes in the ground next to Kirsten's. We collected stones and piled them above the ashes. This activity, satisfying to all of us, was especially engaging for Soren. He enjoyed digging the hole for the ashes, searching for stones in the creek bed and placing them on the cairn.

I was not able to participate as exuberantly as Soren and the others did. For me, there was something about carrying out this one last ritual with Nina's ashes and going to this place which was so special to her, where I had never been, that brought on a quiet inner mood. Silent tears rolled down my cheeks. Later, I wrote a poem capturing this feeling.

JOURNEY INTO NINA'S SPACE

The wind
> *blowing through the midsummer grasses*
> *like through the wisps of your golden-soft hair*

The path
> *turning upwards into the woods*
> *like into your inner sanctuary, secluded and private*

The grass
> *whispering a welcome*
> *like your voice, soothing and pure*

The rocks
> *silently streaming the tales of eternity*
> *like your feet, solidly bearing the songs of the earth*

The trees
> *arching upward into the radiant blue*
> *like your arms, enfolding us in infinite love.*

Nina's final disposition was now complete. Her spirit would go on living in the four places where we chose to bury her ashes: in the woodland garden at Camphill Village Minnesota, at the willow tree on the Hawthorne Valley School grounds, at the accident site, and in the woods on the Elinson's property. Her spirit could not be confined to one space, for her life touched so many.

Profound Love

Later in June, after returning from our pilgrimage, I woke up one morning remembering the letter my sister-in-law had written to us eighteen years earlier upon the birth of her son. Sherry vividly described the profound love she felt for this small being.

The way Sherry had worded this sentiment came back to me now and touched something deep within me. The love I had for my own infant daughter, my firstborn, welled up in me anew. I recalled the upstairs apartment of the old white clapboard house where Dennis and I had lived in Dunkirk, New York, when Nina was born. I remembered one day in the first weeks of her life, washing out soiled baby clothing in the bathroom sink. I made up a simple song about it and sang it to Nina in the Snuggli front pack while I worked. It was such a lovely song, sung with such joy.

I couldn't recapture the song, but the feeling I had when singing it remained to this day. I realized that this intense love continued throughout Nina's life, in spite of the daily challenges that come with child rearing. I longed for a way to continue to give this love to her. The longing became a song that kept singing within me for days.

My love found an outlet while I was caring for three extra children three days a week that summer. I felt compelled to give Soren and his friends Samuel, Sarah, and Lauren experiences worthy of my profound love. I wished to create the most enchanting, joyous, carefree, and adventurous summer possible, maximizing all of the resources in our home and natural surroundings.

We had a large corner lot with a flat, grassy yard and a vegetable garden. In the backyard, Soren had a tree house with a zipline trolley going to the other end of the yard. He also had a sandbox. Cutting through the neighbor's yard, we could get to a woodsy 20-acre park. We wandered from house to yard to garden to woods and back. The children dressed up and played house, picked peas in the garden for snacks, played "The Three Billy Goats Gruff" on the bridge over the stream in the woods, and created castles, roads, and villages in the sandbox. I provided the structure, materials, food, rhymes, and stories to spur their own delightful creativity.

That profound love also gave me patience and empathy for other people. Wherever I went, waiting in the grocery store line or swimming at the beach, I looked at the individuals who came across my path differently. I sensed their uniqueness, how special they were to the people close to them, and how much they would be missed if they were to die. Instead of feeling critical of someone who was different from me, or irritable when people took a long time at the checkout line, I silently poured out acceptance and love in the smile I gave them. It was a new and liberating experience.

Nine Little Children

As the summer progressed, the time came for me to prepare for my new teaching job in the fall. I was filling a new position for a preschool teacher at the Spring Hill Waldorf School. Soren was now ready for kindergarten, so it would work out well for me to take him to kindergarten where I worked. My friend Brenda Haak had been the solo teacher of the kindergarten for seven years, laying the firm foundation for a school to grow. The school board decided it was time to add a second classroom for a small group of preschoolers, hence the need for a new teacher. This classroom would be created next to the existing kindergarten classroom in the lower level of the church in Wayzata, 18 miles west of our house in Golden Valley, where the kindergarten had been the past few years.

Over the summer I shopped at garage sales and thrift stores to furnish the classroom with baskets, shells, dress-up clothes, tablecloths, dishes, silverware, cooking pots, and mixing bowls. As August drew near, I made decisions about purchasing the larger equipment, such as shelves, tables, and chairs. Parent volunteers helped create the new space by painting the two existing cinderblock walls and sewing floor-length pink curtains to cover the other two vinyl accordion-style movable walls. When these were completed, we had to figure out how to get electricity into the corner of the room where I would be cooking and needing lamplight, all from one outlet in the opposite corner.

I was occupied many hours of the day tending to these and many other details of trying to create beauty and practicality in a classroom for little children in a church basement. At the same time I was planning stories, verses, circle games, and daily activities for the nine three-, four-, and five-year-olds who would be in my charge three mornings a week. I also made home visits to each of the children's families.

Many times I was ready to throw up my hands in despair. Why had I taken on this new position? Caring for a few children in my own home during the summer had been a good pace and good balance for me. This summer reverie was coming to an end, but fall energy to tackle the new challenges was not welling up in abundance within me. I had little strength to draw on. I continually had to push myself beyond the limits of my emotional capacities. I felt as if, by taking this job, I had outwardly sentenced myself to prison, while inwardly I was standing at the gate of the beautiful world where Nina dwelled. My sentence was hard to bear because it gave me no chance to try to open the gate. I feared that when I was freed from the sentence, the gate would be forever locked, and I would be left outside, totally bereft.

Cheesecake

Thankfully, I got occasional relief from feeling overwhelmed with responsibility. One day at the end of August, while caring for Soren, Sarah, and Samuel at home, a constant hard rain was falling. I was looking forward to going out to eat with Dennis and Nina's friends from Armstrong High School that evening. They had invited us to join them in celebrating the anniversary of their last farewell evening with Nina a year before.

Soren and his friends were engaged in indoor fantasy play. I got inspired to work in the kitchen as they played. I now had a reason to make the cheesecake I had been thinking about—for the friends I would be seeing that evening. Nina had made cheesecake, a favorite of hers, for her friends on several occasions before. Inwardly I dedicated this day to her, and became gleeful at the purpose behind my whimsy. I cried as I baked, but felt good doing something Nina would have done and living in memories of her for a time, even though it was painful.

The evening at the Mud Pie with Stacy, Shannon, Geri, Sandy, Alexis, and Bethany was a joy. We declined dessert at the restaurant and went to our home to eat strawberry cheesecake together. Most of the girls were packing up to leave for college soon, so we bid them a fond and teary farewell. I was grateful to Nina for her friends and her inspiration for that day, which helped put my life a bit more in perspective.

Autumn

✳

Room Switch

On the Saturday of Labor Day weekend, fifteen-year-old Ciaran, Gwyneth and Annamaria's brother, arrived from Camphill to live with us for the year so he could attend the Youth Initiative High School with Kevin. He had been home schooled and now would be in ninth grade, while Kevin would be in eleventh. His parents brought him and his baggage and drove back to Camphill with the plan that Ciaran would ride the airport limousine to Sauk Centre to be home every weekend.

Dennis, Kevin, and I had spent the previous weeks transforming Kevin's basement room for Ciaran's arrival; they would be sharing the room. We repainted the walls off-white, and removed the gold-colored shag carpet and replaced it with industrial grade brown carpet. We moved Nina's single bed downstairs so that both boys would have a single bed. The extra double bed, the desk, and computer that had been in Kevin's large room came up to Nina's room.

It was only with great reluctance that I endured these

changes. My common sense won out over my emotions in trying to make things work for Ciaran to live with us. Truthfully, however, I was not ready to take Nina's bed away from its rightful place, upsetting the natural order of things. With the bed gone, her room would never be quite the same.

Despite my misgivings, I helped transform Nina's room into a study and guest room. It was time to sort through her other possessions and decide what to use, what to give away, and what to keep as history. I did not want them to be history—mere curiosities from a girl's life that was cut short. I wanted Nina's life to go on.

Dennis and I ended up keeping most of her things until I felt ready to let them go, storing them in her dresser. Nina's postcards remained along the top border of the walls, and her bookshelf and books were still in their place. The canvas duffel bag in the closet still held her clothes that we had shipped home from Harlemville. And Kirsten's painting of the tree with the fairies was still on the wall. We continued to call it "Nina's room."

Amidst the chaos of moving furniture, re-arranging, sweeping, and dusting on Saturday, I wept continuously. Ciaran and Kevin, Dennis and Soren got used to my tears and didn't bother comforting me. By Sunday, August 31, the day when we had said good-bye to Nina and Kirsten the year before, my tears were all gone. There was just a dull ache of sadness in my heart, which left me feeling listless and withdrawn.

On Tuesday, the day before my preschool started, I needed to complete the home visits I was making to all of my preschoolers. Before I left home after lunch,

I took a peaceful nap. I awoke from that nap with the feeling of Nina's deep love for me permeating my being. It complemented the dream I had earlier in the summer when I awoke with the feeling of my profound love for Nina. In this dream, Nina's love originated in the love of daughter to mother, but was striving to become the love of soul to soul.

I felt as if an aura of warmth extended beyond my skin like a comforting invisible mantel. Surely I need never doubt our abiding connection with such proof! The aura of warmth accompanied me throughout that afternoon. Whenever I tuned in to it as I went about my activities, it brought a lift to my heart, replacing the ache.

Melancholy

The fall of 1997 was probably the most difficult time of my life. When I reread my journal I was reminded, with surprise, of all that was going on then. I was coping with a new job at the Spring Hill School and Dennis and I faced challenges at home with an extra teenager. In addition, we had out-of-town visitors for four days in September, and I traveled twice to Bloomington, Indiana, once alone and once with the whole family. Having so many complications in life, while not yet through the first year of my grief, was intense and exhausting.

I continued to feel as if I were living out my "prison sentence" at school, but when I was in the classroom with the children, I felt satisfaction. Singing and playing, baking and painting, celebrating birthdays and seasonal changes with these little ones brought many joys. I felt

burdened, however, by the nightly preparation time, the
30–40 minute commute to and from the school, and
the challenges of working in a new situation with new
colleagues.

After lunch each day, driving home from school with
Soren, I was reminded of my personal situation. Regardless of whether the morning had gone well or not, facing
life with the gaping loss of my daughter and trying to
work as if nothing was wrong or different, was overwhelming. I just wanted to lie down and die. Day after
day I had the same feeling. I didn't have thoughts of
actual suicide; I only had a wish not to live, not to have
to go through this pain.

My brother Alan, his wife, and their three children
came to visit at the end of September on their way
across the country to a new home. With Nina's death,
they had undergone a reevaluation and reprioritizing of
their life, and decided to uproot themselves from their
home in Bristol, Vermont, to carry out a wish to live in
San Francisco.

This was a special visit to us. Although we had visited Alan and Andrea in Vermont several times since
their wedding there in 1984, they had never been to
our home. They had been with us at Nina's wake and
funeral, as well as at the graduation of Nina's class
in Harlemville. Our whole family was happy to have
another time to connect and share our life in Minnesota
with them.

Alan and Andrea had never seen Nina's room. On the
morning after they arrived, I sat on the guest bed with
them, listening to the music of Enya. I bared my soul

and the depth of my despair like I had with no one else. I sobbed as I pulled out every piece of Nina's clothing I had packed away in the duffle bag, one by one, to show to them. They appeared so insignificant—a short flow-ered dress that Nina had bought at a thrift store, a pair of green corduroy pants and flannel shirt that she had worn often in winter, a pair of shoes that held the familiar shape of her foot, a bathing suit, pajama pants—yet they were what I had left of Nina. How could I ever throw or give them away? Alan and Andrea understood how I felt and assured me that I never had to get rid of them.

Later that day both of our families hiked around Min-nehaha Falls and then had a picnic. We celebrated Rylan and Amelia's fall birthdays with cake and ice cream. I revealed in a conversation with Alan and Andrea after-ward that I just couldn't understand why we wished people "joy and long life on earth" in the song that we sang for birthdays. My only wish at the time was to die, and so living a long life sounded like a prison sentence. It seemed like death was far superior. Nina was the one dwelling in a beautiful world, and I wanted to be there with her. It was too hard to live here without her. They did what they could for me—listened and held me close, offering words of sympathy and support.

Our family took Alan, Andrea, and their children to Camphill Village over the weekend. We gave them a walking tour of the houses and farm, introducing them to many people and places that had been part of our lives for five years. We slept in tents on Saturday night and participated in the outdoor Michaelmas festival on Sunday, which included harvesting potatoes and eating vegetable soup cooked in a large kettle over the fire. We were all invigorated by this community experience.

On Monday morning, our family sadly said goodbye to my brother's family as they left for points further west, and we went back to school and work.

The next weekend I was in Bloomington, Indiana, visiting my mother. In July, Mom had been admitted to the Health Pavilion, the area of her retirement residence where people receive round-the-clock health care. By the end of September, she was showing further decline, indicating that death might be imminent.

Two weeks later our whole family made the trip to Bloomington, driving fourteen hours in our minivan. In the time since I had been there, however, my mother had begun to improve instead of continuing to decline.

The two visits with my mother in a nursing home were hard for all of us, but also peaceful, for we no longer had issues to discuss or plans to make. She would most likely spend the rest of her life in the nursing home. We accepted that and just lived in the moment.

In between these two visits, Dennis, Soren, Kevin, Ciaran, and I celebrated Nina's birthday. We approached October 17 in a mood of delicate expectancy, trying to feel our way through to what should be done. In our family year of birthdays, Nina was the last one, so we had all had a birthday without Nina. This was different. Her birthday no longer had the same meaning. She was our eldest, so she had always paved the way, but now she could not teach us what it was like to turn 19 or be out of school at last.

We did our fair share of looking back on Nina's life

in its different stages in our conversations about her birthday. I found myself looking through piles of photos that hadn't been put in albums for glimpses of forgotten memories. This led me to make an album of photos depicting her life chronologically.

A few days ahead of time, Dennis and I spontaneously came up with a plan to honor Nina's birthday. As on the day she died, the urge to include others came to the fore. Ciaran was eager to create an event, and persuaded us to bake a rich chocolate cake. We invited friends to come to our house on October 17 and bring food to share. Kevin and Ciaran invited some high school friends. We had a mix of teens, our middle aged friends (including Linda), as well as Soren, the Pilgrim children and other kids. Our small living room/dining room was full with about 20 people.

We had pushed all of our furniture to the walls, except for the table. After eating the main meal, we gathered together in a big circle to light the candles on Nina's cake. Dennis and I opened the packages that Gwyneth and Laura had sent. We did not sing "Happy Birthday." Instead, I was inspired in the moment to lead our friends in singing a Russian song I remembered learning from Nina. We circled around in a grapevine step while we sang, pulsing with energy radiating out to the universe "providing music for the stars to be dancing circles in the night."

It had been an exhilarating evening. I was grateful to have all those people there with our family to sing and dance, to transform the sorrow we felt on Nina's birthday into an enlivening community experience.

First Anniversary

We came through Nina's birthday month, with the tumultuous events of this particular year, to face what would forever be the month of Nina's death. To remember her birth and death juxtaposed as they were in the calendar year was to confront the riddle of her life and death itself.

My state of soul in November reflected the outer world in its transition to winter. I felt as grey as the sunless skies and as bereft as the trees without their leaves, as I wrote in this poem:

November 28, 1997

> *Oh, joy, thou art as elusive*
> *As the dream of my life!*
> *I feel like the prairie grasses*
> *Which in September shone russet in the sunset,*
> *But by day were drab and dirty.*
> *Perhaps one day I will shine golden above the snow*
> *Even when the day skies*
> *Are filled with November clouds.*

As November drew us closer to the darkest time of the year, I drug my feet through the fog and mist that threatened to envelop me forever, hoping for some light to save me.

Dennis and I knew, as the fated weekend approached, that we needed to be surrounded by the loving embrace of the Camphill community, and close to the Sacred Garden where the spirit of Nina was held in beauty.

Because November 29 fell on the Saturday after Thanksgiving, Linda planned to be with the O'Brien family at their home in northern Wisconsin, so we wouldn't be together. I contacted Lois Smith about having a gathering at Camphill Village. Lois and others were enthusiastic about us coming there. Lois prepared the choir to sing a piece of music with words by William Penn.

Our family went to Camphill on the 29th and joined many people from the Village for the gathering in the festival hall at 7:00 PM. After words of remembrance and the choir piece, we all took candles, bundled up in our winter coats and boots, and trundled down the path covered with fresh snow across the little bridge to the Sacred Garden. Once there, we stood in a circle, as we did when we spread Nina's ashes six months before, lit our candles and sang a round that illumined the dark night along with our candles.

At the conclusion, everyone walked back to their houses in silence, keeping their candles lit for as long as possible.

Although the fact of Nina's death a year ago still felt unreal, this dreaded day became for us an uplifting celebration of her spirit, present in a tangible way in community with others.

The uplifted mood of the weekend continued with the Advent Garden the next evening. Even after we left Camphill our family traditionally participated in this event, which usually occurred on the Sunday after Thanksgiving. It was a highlight of the year for us. The choir sang and a small ensemble of recorder and lyre music played to accompany the children walking the

evergreen spiral. Nina had loved being one of the singers after she was too old to walk the spiral.

This year, Dennis, Kevin, and I watched Soren as he
walked the spiral. I tried to sing along with the others,
but tears overcame me most of the time.

When the Advent Garden was over, Angela Briggs,
a teenager currently living at Camphill who knew Nina
from her visits to the Village, came up to me with a
beaming smile on her face. She presented me with a
poem she had written the night before. This capped the
weekend for me, filling my heart with a deep, rejuvenat-
ing joy. The poem ended with these words:

> *I know that you are often watching over us,*
> *And that your spirit is with us all,*
> *During this special time of year.*
> *Tonight I really noticed you looking down on us,*
> *And I could feel your Being around us.*
> *Not until this evening did I really see*
> *The true beauty of all that is around me.*
> *Thank you for opening my eyes and my soul.*

This poem confirmed what I had felt at the gathering.
Nina would continue to be remembered, not only as the
friend who was lost, but as the friend who continued to
touch lives with love, protection, and inspiration from
the Spirit realm.

The next week, I returned to my work at Spring Hill
with renewed energy. As the other teachers and I prepared our Light Festival (another name for the Advent
Garden celebrated a week later for the children at the
school), the tranquility of the weekend carried me. I was

able to work more harmoniously with my coworkers and transcend the earlier tensions that were challenging. It was a turning point for me and I felt at peace with my school situation.

I could then assure my brother Alan, who had been concerned about my mental health after our conversation in September, that I would be okay without any intervention. I no longer felt overcome by the wish to die. My experience at the threshold, still very immediate, was filling me with light. I had teetered precariously at the brink of the abyss, but by accepting it and talking about it I found my way to the other side.

PART III

Healings

Winter

While under the spell of the spiritual abundance I experienced at the year anniversary, I thought I was on my way to healing and that the light I experienced could not be dimmed. However, life moves on, the seasons change, and new emotional events come into the picture. Though Christmas is a festival of light and a spiritual celebration, it is also a highly charged emotional event tied to family and rituals. I wrote in my journal on December 25, 1997, about the new emotions that came with this season and threatened my newfound equilibrium.

Before Christmas ever came, I was filled with light. But then human weakness intervened and dimmed that light so that it could not radiate. At first this was devastating and sorrow took the upper hand. Then sorrow left and I was only numb; numb to sorrow or joy. For me, to not weep is to be numb. I know that I must stop weeping, for Kevin and Soren especially. But can I be filled with light

without also weeping? And when will I be ready to die—
when the light cannot be overcome by human weakness?
Or when I have learned to be happy being numb?

The next year, 1998, was filled with these ups and downs
as the space between the present and the most fateful
event of our lives lengthened. There were times when
I felt like all my energy was being used up in surviv-
ing and coping. Sometimes I felt like a physical wreck,
overwhelmed, and unable to cope. Other times I felt like
revolting at life getting back to normal without Nina
being a part of it. Occasionally, I was filled with the joy
of Nina's presence in the fire of a new inspiration.

There came a Thursday in March when I did not get
out of bed. I was not sick. I told Kevin he could drive the
car to school because I would not need it, and I told Dennis to take Soren to school and go to the Reading for the
Dead group without me. Never before had I done this.

When everyone left, it got unfamiliarly quiet. I just
lay on the bed in Nina's room and cried. It felt so good
to lay there with no expectations. I fantasized about
what I could do next. The fantasies ranged from lying
in bed for the whole day, to calling my co-teacher to tell
her I couldn't come in for the rest of the year, to going to
India to work with lepers.

I latched onto this idea of going far away for a long
period of time, taking nothing with me but clothes, a
journal, and writing materials. No photos. No books.
Not even Nina's journal. I wrote in my journal:

Everything that I am I would have to hold in my heart.
Perhaps then I would hurt more than I do now. Perhaps
I would hurt enough to help other people, for that would
be all I could do with whatever love I had left in me.
Perhaps I would hurt bad enough, to come back and be a
good wife and mother.

Soon enough, Dennis and Soren came back for lunch.
I got up and ate with them. Dennis went to work and
a neighbor friend came to play with Soren. I played
a game with them. I decided I had better go back to
school the next day. I thought about going away in the
fall, instead of returning to teaching. But I didn't really
come up with a plan to act on my fantasies.

Three days later, I woke up with the great weight that
had been bearing down on me for weeks lifted from my
shoulders. I felt happy. This feeling did not have anything to do with outer events; I just started the day off
with an inner feeling of freedom—no cloud to keep my
light from shining.

This mood lasted for about three weeks. In this
period, I only cried once. Up until that time I had cried
every day. This inner strength carried me through a
weekend when I visited my mother in Bloomington,
Indiana. My brother and stepfather needed support
in dealing on a daily basis with the frustrations of my
mother in the nursing home. Her ability to do even the
simplest tasks for herself was declining. She continued
to lose weight and her state of mental confusion was
becoming a greater and greater percentage of her total

mental function. Visiting her every day or every week was a grim task for Wayne and Eric.

I attempted to shed some positive light on the situation from my spiritual perspective and experience at Camphill. I had lived with people whom others would consider beyond hope and of no good to anyone. Camphill nurtures respect for every individual and the contribution each one makes to the community. It acknowledges the spark of the divine in every human being. I suggested that, in elderly people, though they may lose some of their former physical or mental capacities, there is still something that they have to offer those around them. "Quality of life" is not something that we can judge or measure only by material standards.

After a day of trying to keep everyone else buoyed up during this visit, I was struck by a wave of my own personal grief. I went out into the evening air, walking on the lovely grounds of the retirement center. No one was around, so I gave free reign to my sobbing. When it subsided, I came in to say goodnight to my mother. She was already bedded down for the night. I sat down next to the bed and sang to her, for I knew she was not truly sleeping yet. My love for my mother and for my daughter, both worlds away from me, came gushing out in weeping again. This caused my mother to open her eyes and look at me in a true meeting of soul to soul. She reached out to me and said, "Just go ahead and cry." I lay my head on her shoulder and felt embraced by her. That was the mother that I knew and remembered.

This rare lucid moment, brief as it was, connected

me with my mother once again. Her spirit was still alive inside her ailing body and demented mind! Eric, Wayne, nor I would never know what was getting through to her, but we could not assume that "she" wasn't there.

I saw my mother as a queen in her wheelchair throne. Attendants carried out her every need without her even asking. She never demanded anything, but courteously received the services she was given. She had no interest in the material world, so she only needed the necessary comforts of life.

After a life of serving others, my mother surrendered herself to being served. She sacrificed her life, her golden years in retirement with a new husband, and all worldly concerns, to the journey toward the spiritual world.

Getaway

Just as night follows day, and then day comes again, a time of darkness followed this period of light, but an even longer period of light emerged.

Once again, our family went to Camphill Village to celebrate Easter. Dennis and I joined the hardy souls who got up on Easter morning for a sunrise service in a field by the river. It was very windy and cold out on the open hills at 6:00 AM. By Sunday evening, I had a sore throat and Dennis had swollen glands.

Kevin was spending spring break at Camphill with his friends Nic and Ciaran. Dennis and I had planned to leave Soren with the Leighton family so we could have a "getaway" at a bed and breakfast north of Long Prairie. Something came up for the Leightons, and they were not able to care for Soren, so we had to cancel our reservations. We left Kevin there, drove back to Minneapolis, and got on the phone to devise a new plan. I was determined to make this first getaway since Nina died happen, even though we were feeling sick! Thankfully, Kim Pilgrim was willing to take Soren for the next two and a half days.

On Monday morning, we dropped Soren off at Kim's and drove forty minutes east to Stillwater, Minnesota. We found a third floor room with a Jacuzzi in a pleasant turn-of-the-century inn. Still feeling sick, we fell into bed for the next 16 hours. During that long night, our symptoms cleared up and we let the rapture of love take over. This deep sexual intimacy was healing balm for a husband and wife who had been engulfed in pain and grief for a year and a half.

When we woke at nine the next morning, we went downstairs to the dining room for breakfast with two other couples. One couple was so interested in our life circumstance that they came upstairs to a lounge area, where we sat and talked for two hours. They wanted to know what it was like to lose a child. There was something very special about sharing our experience with these strangers.

The Jacuzzi, the weather, the romantic ambience of the river town, and the lavish breakfasts all contributed to our well being. Dennis and I wandered around Stillwater in the balmy early spring weather. We ate delicious meals in restaurants. We sat on the porch of the inn and enjoyed watching children coming home from school. We read as much as we wanted to.

After two romantic nights away, I felt as if the wound

caused by Nina's sudden death had healed. To feel in love again enabled my husband and me to turn a corner. Or was it the other way around—because our wound was healed, we were able to feel in love again? By immersing ourselves in the sensual, we burst out of the bubble we had been suspended in. Our feet were on the earth now; we were free to experience physical existence to the fullest.

My heart rejoiced at every thought of Nina's release from the bondage to the earth that our grief had caused her. I was no longer catapulted into wrenching pain when I missed Nina or felt sad. I no longer felt the same kind of exhaustion in the evenings. I began to sleep better and feel better in my body. Once more, I felt hopeful about life.

Stories

Our family and Linda Bergh traveled to Harlemville again in June of 1998 for what would have been Kirsten's graduation. It was less intense for us than the previous year's graduation of Nina's class.

On this visit, Dennis and I were not looking at the past as much as forward. We wanted to see if there was a future for us in the Harlemville community. This was a serious question. We felt drawn to the community because of its connection to Nina, and now we were trying to determine objectively if there was any other reason for us to move there. After some exploration of possibilities, we decided it was okay to close that door for now.

In another way, the trip was valuable to me. While

there, I wrote a story about Nina's relationship to her grandma (Oma). I made it into a handwritten book illustrated with photographs, and drew a picture on the cover. I was exhilarated by this artistic endeavor. It helped me process the double loss that I was experiencing with my mother's decline.

I gave the book as a gift to Sarah Elinson, Zusha's sister, whom I had met along with her grandmother on that last visit with Nina in Harlemville. She had devotedly written postcards to us every few months over the year and a half since Nina's death. I wanted to return the gesture of interest and kindness. At a last meal at the Elinson's, I gave it to her and we looked through it together. She appreciated getting to know Nina and her family better.

NINA AND OMA

Nina was the first grandchild in my family. Not only was she my mother's first grandchild, but also my grandfather's first great-grandchild. He got to see Nina before he died when she was a few months old. "Too sweet for the world," said he and Grandma Audrey (my step-grandmother).

I was overjoyed when my firstborn turned out to be a girl. My mother felt that way, too. She flew out to Dunkirk, New York from Indianapolis on the day she was born and stayed for two weeks. We gave her the name Oma right away because we liked the short and affectionate German version of grandmother, and so that she wouldn't be confused with the other grandma. That's what Nina and Kevin and Soren have always called her.

Oma spent a few of her retirement years alone in

Indianapolis. She taught English as a second language, read a lot, and still sewed a few things for her grandchildren—including clothes for Nina's "Kirsten" doll. In these years she also went on her last backpacking trips. A few years later she was to pass on her hiking boots to Nina!

Then she moved to Hawaii because she fell in love with my dad's cousin, Wayne, who lived there. (Nina never knew my dad—he died when I was 17.) We had one glorious vacation there when Nina was thirteen. My mother had already been diagnosed with Parkinson's, but the symptoms were still very mild, so she and Wayne had a great time showing us around. They married in 1994.

In August of 1996, after she and Wayne had moved back to Indiana, Oma stayed with us for a week while Wayne visited his daughter in Alaska. By this time, Oma was much less able to function on her own, but we still took neighborhood walks with her, she with a cane. Oma was not always coherent, and she tired easily. Nonetheless, we dragged her along on a few shopping trips to buy clothes and supplies for Nina to go away to school in New York.

Oma told us on this visit that she would like to contribute some money for Nina's tuition at Hawthorne Valley. I was pleased when she later came through with this, for I wasn't sure at the time if she knew what she was saying. But it was so typical of her to be generous and supportive of what her children or grandchildren deemed important.

On that last visit, Nina and Oma laughed a lot together. This was the hallmark of their relationship. When Nina started giggling about the words or expressions Oma used or some frustration she was having, she got Oma laughing at herself. They showed their acceptance of and love for each other through their laughter.

Nina left home with Oma's sense of adventure, beauty, and optimism carrying her. Fearlessly she entered a new school in an unknown community, and joyously she met her sudden death.

Nina's destiny seems strangely intertwined with Oma's. After Nina's death, Oma's physical and mental health deteriorated rapidly. Just eight months later she was admitted to the nursing home at age 75. She lives from day to day as if in a dream. Only very occasionally do we get a momentary glimpse of her higher self.

Now we are learning how to accept and love Nina and Oma for who they are in their new dwelling places.

When I completed this book, I thought I had written the last story about Nina. I felt sad and devastated at this finality. I had a similar feeling after completing the scrapbooks with photos of Nina. I had seen all the photographs of Nina there were to see. There would never be any new ones, and the old ones would look yellowed and outdated.

Later that summer, I was proved wrong. In July, Linda shared with me the letters that Nina had written to Kirsten when she was 13, 14, and 15 years old. These included the two letters that Nina wrote to Kirsten while she lived in France, parts of which are in Part I of this book. The stories were not all exhausted!

Dennis and I felt privileged to read these letters. They revealed to us the intimate soul life of our 14-year-old daughter. We were filled with wonder at this new perspective on Nina's inner being. I humbly realized that, as quick to criticize her appearance as I had been, she had an exquisite sense of her own inner beauty.

Another Birthday

In September 1998, Nina's Camphill friends, Gwyneth and Annamaria, came to live in Minneapolis for a year. Gwyneth stayed at Linda's house and worked at a bakery. Annamaria lived with a family in Linden Hills and helped with their children.

We agreed to have supper together once a week when possible. Most weeks, Gwyneth and Annamaria managed to come to our house. Kevin was often absent for these meals, as he was busy acting in the senior play at school, playing his cello in the Greater Twin Cities Youth Symphony, and working on his senior project. When we were all there, we felt like a family. Dennis and I appreciated hearing the weekly chatter from these young women in their early twenties, the same age our own daughter would have been.

Dennis and I wondered how we should celebrate Nina's second birthday after her death. Linda, Molly O'Brien, Gwyneth, and Annamaria came up with an idea inspired by a protest against a proposed highway expansion in south Minneapolis that would destroy wooded land and a freshwater spring sacred to the Lakota people. Some of the protestors camped out on the land, right in the city. They were accepting donations of food to help sustain their presence.

The idea was to get together on Nina's birthday to make some food to take to the protestors. Three of Kevin's classmates (including Molly), as well as Gwyneth, Annamaria, and our whole family, met at Linda's house at 4:30 on October 17 to prepare chili and apple crisp and have a snack. When the food was done, we took it to the encampment near Minnehaha Park, although it was already dark.

The Native Americans and their supporters at the encampment had a tent where food was set out. They welcomed our contribution of warm chili and apple crisp. The ten of us stood around talking with the people there. The longer we stayed, the more our hosts talked to us. At last, a well-spoken Lakota man in his 30's, dressed in western clothing, invited us to come into the tipi where their sacred fire was kept burning. First he instructed us about tipi and sweat lodge etiquette. We all found a seat on the ground around the warm fire, walking clockwise around the circle, and not walking in front of anyone. He shared with us many aspects of Lakota philosophy, especially about the role of and respect for the feminine and how it was reflected in concern for the environment. He spoke powerfully. We felt honored to have been so richly repaid for our small contribution.

At 8:00, we returned to the Bergh/O'Brien house to have dinner around a candlelit table. After the chili, we sang and ate cheesecake, Nina's favorite dessert, in her honor. The youth were ignited by our contact with the people involved in the highway protest.

We were pleased with this birthday celebration, so different from the one just a year earlier. We had turned what could have been a sad day into an inspiring event. Honoring Nina through an act of service gave her birthday new meaning, far beyond anything I could have dreamed.

At the Threshold

Thresholds Remembered

We spent the Christmas of 1998 at Camphill house-sitting in Oakwood House while the Potter family was on vacation. It was an unusual experience to be in someone else's house at Christmas with their tree and decorations. Our former housemate, Evelyn, was the only person with special needs remaining in Oakwood over the holidays. We carried on with our traditions to the extent that we were able to fit them to a new situation and include Evelyn.

It also was a memorable Christmas because Soren had the chickenpox. He had started to get spots the day we left home, December 22, but he didn't feel sick until the second day we were there. When we arrived he went ice skating on the Marlspring pond with Kevin and some other children in the Village. After that, he stayed at home.

We had looked forward to being in Camphill to participate in the many special Christmas traditions in the community, but as circumstance would have it, one of us always had to stay at home with Soren. I went to the performance of the annual Shepherd's Play on December 23 while Dennis stayed with Soren, and Dennis went to the midnight service and singing to the cows on Christmas Eve while I stayed home. Though the chickenpox limited our activities, we were happy to be at Camphill where friends could easily stop in to visit and we could still experience the seasonal cheer.

Soren's worst night of itching was Christmas Eve. He had trouble sleeping. At 2 AM I put him in a baking soda bath to relieve the itching. After that he was able to sleep, and Santa Claus had a chance to deliver presents under the Christmas tree.

Soren got up to open his presents from Santa and played with his new finger puppets and farm/village set for a little while before he tired again. Kevin had stayed with Ciaran at Prairie Wind, the Village house where the Leighton family lived. He came home for Christmas dinner. The rest of the Leighton family and Lois Smith also joined us for dinner and singing Christmas carols afterward.

We stayed at Camphill until December 28. After Christmas, the community celebrates the Twelve Holy Nights with gatherings at dusk around the large candlelit tree in the Hall. Each house community plans and leads the gathering for one night. This year the theme was "thresholds."

The gathering we attended on December 26 got me to thinking about thresholds. Our family had the obvious experiences at the threshold of birth with the home births of our three children, as well as the threshold of death with Nina's crossing. As I looked back on the year, I recalled the times when I had experienced healing, or spirit birth. I saw these as threshold experiences, when I felt the nearness of the spiritual world.

Our family's trip to the North Shore the summer before, with our hike up to the waterfall and the spontaneous decision to step into the waterfall, offered a good metaphor for a threshold experience. The courage to cross from dry air, comfort, and the known, into the wet and pounding unknown of the waterfall came suddenly, in a moment. But once I crossed the threshold, I was there in an instant, in the cascading water, and a torrent of joy and laughter was unleashed.

Because it happened so quickly, I cannot trace the steps that led me to cross that threshold. Had I decided not to enter the waterfall, I would have stayed warm, dry, and comfortable. But I would not have been the recipient of that moment of grace.

Two great thresholds stand at the beginning and end of life. At one end, a soul is incarnating, entering earthly life in a physical body. At the other end, the physical body is left behind and the soul expands again into its heavenly home. In between, there are many moments when we hover at thresholds between the world of earth and the world of spirit. The sacred times when I am aware of the closeness of the two worlds give meaning to my life. Birth, death, and other moments at the threshold have become the script of the cosmic drama in which my soul finds its true expression.

Departure

In June of 1999, we stood at another threshold: Kevin's graduation from the Youth Initiative, now named Watershed High School. It was not a what-would-have-been-graduation, but a real one—a rite of passage for our eldest son. A few weeks after graduation, Kevin would be leaving the country, going to Eastern Europe on tour with the Greater Twin Cities Youth Symphony, and then to Germany to work for a year on a farm. Though Dennis and I supported him in these choices, we struggled with this dramatic departure. One part of us was happy for his emancipation from us; another part grieved over the loss his leaving would bring. He would be so far away, with no chance of coming home for a visit for a long time.

The anticipation of saying goodbye to Kevin was bound up with grief over losing Nina before she graduated. Would Kevin's departure plunge me back into the abyss of despair?

At the many graduation events preceding the actual goodbye, there were moments of swelling pride and love, celebration, and friendship. Kevin's graduation was the climax of many more years than high school, for his class included dear family friends, three of whom we had known since preschool, including Molly O'Brien, and another since first grade.

At the graduation ceremony of his class of twelve, we took our places near the front. The moment I looked at the program, I fell apart, for I saw that Kevin and Molly O'Brien were to dedicate the class gift to the school.

The graduating class had decided to give money to the Nina and Kirsten Memorial Fund of Watershed High School, but Kevin hadn't told us that he would be speaking. Near the beginning of the ceremony, the graduating students passed out roses to each parent. That rose saved me from total breakdown. When I felt like crying, I stuck my nose in the rose, and its delicate scent drove away the tears. Thus, I was able to savor every moment.

When Kevin and Molly's turn came, they stood together and spoke with admirable uprightness about the greatest loss of their life. I think everyone in the audience was holding his/her breath through this presentation. Neither Molly nor Kevin shed tears as they spoke, but their words held more intense emotion than those of more sentimental speakers from the class.

A week later, on the night before Kevin's departure, we had our farewell dinner at home. I cooked a feast to please Kevin: apples 'n onions, meatloaf, mashed potatoes, and sauerkraut. Spending a whole evening with Kevin was a rare privilege in those packed days. We were also pleased to have Gwyneth and Bethany, who both happened to be in town, join us. We ate inside, and then went to the backyard to crank homemade ice cream, which we ate on top of gingerbread.

Later, Kevin and Bethany worked on a puzzle with Soren, while Dennis, Gwyneth, and I sat and talked. It was so congenial and homey. Having Gwyneth and Bethany there gave us the joyful feeling of having a big sister home to see Kevin off, of being a whole family.

The climax of all the grief-in-anticipation came when Dennis and I actually took Kevin to the airport

Kevin, Dennis, Marianne, and Soren at the airport, June 1999

and watched him go through the door onto the plane.
All I could think of was the moment when we gave
our last wave to Nina as she boarded the plane to New
York. We never dreamed she would not come home
again. Would Kevin come home? What calamities
might befall him on his travels? Dennis and I tried to
hide our tears from Soren and Kevin. We didn't dare
voice our unspeakable fears.

After Kevin left for Europe, I got caught up in planning a party for Soren's seventh birthday on June 20.
We had invited seven children for the party, which was
to happen three days later, but we didn't have anything
planned besides cake and ice cream. I hit on a fairy tale

theme, and off I went in a flurry of inspiration, creating costumes, games, and prizes. This was a blessing, for the anticipated mourning had little chance to surface. Actually, with Kevin's departure, Dennis and I experienced a surprising feeling of freedom from responsibility. We still had Soren at home, so we didn't feel complete emancipation, but to no longer be involved on a day-to-day basis in the life of an 18-year-old was a relief.

Kevin, however, didn't call or send even a postcard during his ten day Eastern European Youth Symphony tour. Finally, when he had arrived at his new home in Germany, he called.

The tour had gone well and he had enjoyed it immensely. His new situation on the Patersberghhof in the village of Veitlahm in northern Bavaria was congenial. He lived on the third floor above a Waldorf school with a family with one ten-year-old boy still at home. He helped the farmer, Alwin, with their very small dairy operation.

After that, we had regular contact with Kevin. He was a bit lonely for the first few weeks. He let us know how much he appreciated hearing from us, either by letter or phone call. We felt needed. As he got accustomed to speaking German, his home and work situation kept improving; he was making friends and enjoying his work. For Dennis and me, the joy of knowing that Kevin was doing well eased the pain of separation.

A touch of melancholy occasionally wafted in the warm summer breezes, and a tinge of grey sometimes darkened the fluffy clouds of our pride in successfully graduating Kevin, but thankfully, our parachute floated gently to the far side of the dreaded abyss.

Last Visit

Soon after Kevin left for Europe, I went to Bloomington to visit my mother. Alan visited there at the same time I did in early July. In May, Eric and Sherry had taken my mother out of the nursing home to care for her at home. She was nearing the end of her life, and they wanted to give her more personal care in their home surroundings. We three siblings wanted to be together with her before she died. Alan and I also wanted to offer support to Eric and Sherry in their care giving.

I returned to Minneapolis with thoughts of my mom, and Eric and Sherry's devoted care for her, constantly on my mind. It was hard to be a daughter so far away, not to be there to help ease the burden for the caregivers, or to know the daily ups and downs of her condition.

Soon after I got home, I started a series of Rolfing sessions. Rolfing, also known as Structural Integration, is a form of deep-tissue massage that helps to restructure poor posture and bring the body into better balance and alignment. I sought out this bodywork for relief from some chronic health issues. Little did I know how intense and painful it would be! These traumatic weekly sessions touched and brought to consciousness emotions stored deep in my body. After the first session, I spent the next day processing all that had come up, and wrote this poem.

FOR MY MOM

Not in fetal position do you lie,
But stiff and straight from the hips up,
Yet limp as a washrag
Lying there waiting
To have something done to you or not,
Lying there waiting
To have your body pushed one way or another
And all you can do is accept what is given.

You do not retreat in cowardice
To the womb of your childhood
But bear it all upright,
Face ever outward turned
As reflects your stance in life:
Strong and courageous,
Uncomplaining.

Lying here like you,
As my body gets pushed and pulled,
I weep, (as you sometimes do),
For you, and all the pain that has been.
I am wrestling, for I am still a part of life,
But you are letting go,
Unraveling the threads,
Peeling away the years,
Until there is nothing left but you,
Nothing but love caring for what is left of your body
Nothing but love beckoning to you from above
Nothing but love connecting me to you
As I lie here, helpless.

The realization that my mother soon would be transitioning cut through many layers of protection and pierced the core of my being, already wounded by my other losses. I was left exposed and vulnerable.

Final Farewell

Our family did not plan any trips for the summer as we waited for the call to tell us that my mother was actively dying. We had a placid, contented kind of summer because we didn't think much about what was coming next, but lived each day as it came. Going to Soren's "pitch by coach" baseball games was a new and pleasurable pastime several evenings a week. We also watched a few St. Paul Saints baseball games, saw Shakespeare in the park, and savored other cultural amenities of the Twin Cities.

At the end of July, we went on a four day camping trip to get out of the city at least once in the summer. We went south so we would be on our way to Indiana, should we need to go there. We took a set of dress clothes for each of us. On Monday, we called Eric and Sherry and learned my mother was semi-comatose. Sherry said that if we wanted to be there for her passing, we should come. We cut our camping trip short and drove all day Monday to Indiana. When we were two hours from Bloomington at about 6:30 PM, we stopped at a park to call Eric and Sherry. Eric told Dennis that my mother had taken her last breath an hour before.

When Dennis gave me the message, tears smarted in my eyes. My mother had died. It sounded so dramatic.

But it wasn't. I knew that she simply had stopped breathing, there in her quiet room in Eric and Sherry's comfortable old house. Somberly, we drove on to Bloomington.

When we arrived, Eric and Sherry were going about their normal household activities, while my mom lay in the family room where she had been for three months. Eric had called the doctor, who had said to wait until business hours the next morning to contact the funeral home. Eric and Sherry invited us to go in and see my mom's body, but left us to ourselves.

Dennis and I took Soren's hands and walked into the family room. Evening sunlight filled the room with a soft glow. We had prepared Soren for what he might see, reminding him of his visit to Paul Bergh in his meditation hut after he had died. The photos of my mother from one month ago, however, did not prepare Soren and Dennis for how emaciated she was, and Dennis whispered, "She is so thin." Soren was quiet, but observant.

My mother lay on her back on the hospital bed with a hospital gown on and a sheet pulled up to her shoulders. Her mouth was open, her closed eyes and cheeks sunken. Her short fluffy gray hair fell away from her face, exposing her broad forehead and large, old ears. Her spirit hovered peacefully around her. Clearly, it was time for her to leave her fragile body and be freed from her suffering.

After I put Soren to bed upstairs, I sat in a chair beside my mother for a time of meditation, sending her thoughts of love on the journey she was beginning. The next morning I awoke early and went to her again. Impulsively, I took pencil and paper and sketched her profile, so stark, so fierce, reflecting her suffering in the last years. Soon she would be wheeled out of the house to the hearse, to be transported by strangers to the funeral home where she would await her cremation. While I wished for more ritual with her body over the next three days, I was grateful that the timing had worked out so I was at least able to see her and bid a last farewell to her physical presence.

My mother died on August 3, 1999, one day short of 30 years after my father's passing on August 4, 1969. The mysterious working of destiny hovered over us like the silent blessing of a magnificent sunset.

Gathering In

Kevin was in Germany when his grandmother died, just as I was in Germany when my father died in 1969. Dennis and I called Kevin on Wednesday morning to tell him of her death and the plan for a memorial service on Saturday. He was not surprised that Oma had died, and took the news matter-of-factly. Having been in Germany for only a month, he did not want to come back for the service. He was caught up in his new life there and, he informed us, his new girlfriend. This was exciting news. We were sad, however, that he would miss the gathering of many relatives whom he had not met or didn't remember.

My father's untimely death years earlier had been a more dramatic experience. He had had several strokes at the age of 46, when I was 15. He never recovered full use of his left side, nor was he able to go back to work as a salesman for the Santa Fe Railroad. When I left for

Krefeld, Germany, two years later, no one expected his death. I participated in the Indiana University Honors Program in Germany for eight weeks from early June to early August. He had a sudden fatal stroke several days before the end of my program. My mother called the director of the program in Germany, and the two of them decided not to tell me until the night before I was to come home.

My German Vati (father) informed me of my father's death with the words, "Dein Vati ist tod," and I broke into tears saying, "Nein, Nein!" I was devastated by the news. I felt guilty for not being home with him before he died. I had a miserable flight home, got sick to my stomach, and cried with my best friend beside me. I didn't think anyone besides my best friend knew the tragedy that had befallen me. I avoided farewells to the good friends I had made over the summer.

By the time I arrived home, the funeral for my father in his hometown, St. Louis, Missouri, had already taken place. I had no chance to say goodbye to him or mourn publicly with the rest of the family. My aunt and uncle were at our home for a day, but when they left, life went on as usual for my family.

Later in August, my mother took me to choose a new Steinway piano with money that we suddenly had. I was a serious piano student, and was thrilled to have a new studio piano with good tone and action to replace the old mediocre upright I had practiced on for years. Was it a way to appease me for having missed the funeral? Was it a dream of my mother's that she could finally fulfill? I don't know. I don't think my two brothers got anything special from our father's insurance benefit. In October, Mom went on a two week trip to the Oregon coast with her parents, leaving us three children at home alone. We were 14, 17, and 20. I don't remember any attention being paid to our grief.

My father's death wounded my child's heart, and the wound oozed within with no one tending to it. I felt like I bore the stigma of an orphan, something that was neither acknowledged nor talked about by either my peers or the adults in my life. Although I had a boyfriend for the first time, which filled a need for love and attention, and threw myself into my piano playing, I did not have a happy senior year in high school. Friends in my old crowd were going their separate ways. I was ready to go on to college.

By the time I was twenty-six, I had given birth to Nina, but I had never seen a dead person or gone to a funeral that I remembered. I felt odd about this, given that my own father had died. Three months after Nina was born, my grandfather died from a heart attack. Dennis and I took Nina to the funeral in Greenville, Pennsylvania. Seeing my grandpa's dead body in the coffin at the front of the church from the balcony where I was sitting was an emotional experience for me, bringing up the buried pain surrounding my father's passing ten years before.

Two years later, newly pregnant with Kevin, I left Dennis at home with Nina and traveled to St. Louis with my brother Eric when my father's brother, my Uncle David, died. Experiencing his funeral gave me some idea of what my father's funeral might have been like. While there, Eric and I went to see my father's gravesite. I hadn't previously been to the cemetery. Connecting with my relatives and experiencing the physical reality of my father's death by being where his body was buried, in lieu of seeing him after he died, helped to begin healing the wound. At least it was no longer oozing.

My next experience with death was more direct. I helped care for a friend, Sarah, who was in the last stages of breast cancer. Her estranged husband, Bob, who had come back to help with her and their children at the end, called me one morning after the children were off to school to tell me that he had found Sarah dead in her bed. He asked me to come over. I called Dennis at work and asked him to come, too. He had worked as an orderly in a hospital and had some experience with dead bodies. I was apprehensive going without him, but went anyway. I could at least be a comforting presence for Bob. I was afraid to go near Sarah's body and kept my distance until Dennis arrived. Soon, Bob called the Cremation Society, finding the number in the yellow pages. Nothing had been planned beforehand, so with only our common sense as our guide, we helped him figure out what to do. An hour later, the Cremation Society came and took her body away.

Ten years later, when Paul Bergh died, Dennis and I and our circle of friends had gained life experience and spiritual perspective. We knew that we had choices for dealing with Paul's body. We wanted to surround this life event with human warmth and spiritual awareness. Having a three day wake at home, with no embalming of the body, was new for all of us, but this ritual/procedure set a precedent. When Nina and Kirsten died, there was no question of what to do. Dennis, Linda, and I had our experience with Paul to draw on. Fortunately, our friends in Harlemville were also experienced in these rites of passage and supported us in carrying out our wishes.

My increasing consciousness around death with each of these events has been an evolving spiritual journey. It was with this wealth of inner resources that I met my mother's death.

Life Cycles

The three deaths in my immediate family have shown me three different ways that life on earth can unfold and come to completion. No one way is the way life should proceed. Each of these ways has a corresponding expression in nature.

A flower, when it is just a bud, clings tenaciously to the stalk. Plants are designed to sustain life under an array of adverse conditions—the usual fluctuations of weather. But unusual conditions, such as the mighty wind of a violent storm, could blow it off the mother plant. Its life is cut short when it is at its most tender beauty. This is how Nina died. Nobody got to see how the blossom would unfold.

Other buds come to flower in their full beauty, are pollinated, and begin to set a fruit containing the seeds for another life. A flower can be blown off while it is in full bloom, leaving the fruit behind. This is how my father died.

Other buds live out the whole life cycle of the plant; they bloom, they set their fruit, gradually wither away, and fall off. This is how my mother died. By the time she took her last breath, she was as withered away as a lily that has slowly lost its vitality, shrivels up, and eventually drops to the ground.

My Mother

After the initial tearful reaction, I did not cry again about my mom dying. My brothers shed more tears than I did at the memorial service. Was something wrong with me? Had I become hardened to death? In a way, this was true. It was nothing like the shock of losing Nina only two and a half years before. For me Nina's loss still eclipsed all others.

The death of an older person after an extended illness is experienced so differently from that of a young person in an accident. In my mother's case, our family had eight years to prepare for her death from the first diagnoses of Parkinson's disease. By the time her death actually came, it was a welcome relief.

Nina's violent, accidental death immediately threw us into questioning, "Why?" We had to feel our way into the essence and meaning of her short life. By the time my mother died, there were no more whys. I could look back at her life with gratitude, for she had already made her impact. Her life's story had been told and felt complete. It didn't need interpretation. My mother's story could be told from many perspectives. As her only daughter, I had a unique perspective. In my quiet moments after she died, I wrote down some things my mother did for me that made a difference in my life. I shared some of them at the memorial service.

My mother served as a role model. She was the essence of "motherliness," providing warmth, love, and security when she welcomed me home from school every day. She was a wealth of creativity, always having a game or project up her sleeve to keep us children resourceful. She taught me basic life skills, like knitting and sewing, which gave me the empowering feeling that I could make what I needed. She had an artistic sense and kept a "beauty spot" in our home; a place that was free of household clutter and could include fresh flowers, a piece of pottery, or a Japanese doll.

My mother recognized my musical inclinations and found a piano teacher who taught me true musicianship. She took me to ballets and concerts when I was in high school, cultivating my own artistic sense. She defied stereotypes in pursuit of her lifelong love of swimming, hiking, and backpacking. She also knew how to enjoy a lazy summer day, sitting in her chaise lounge on the patio with iced coffee in hand, reading a good book.

A social worker by training, she carried out her professional life as a family therapist with grace and integrity. I loved seeing her get dressed up for work, and hearing her professional voice when I called her at work. She was a continual support to me as I grew into adulthood, trusting always that I would make decisions that were right for me. She was a beloved aunt to several of my cousins, who also treasured her supportive role in their lives.

I carry a part of my mother's story in me. It is stored in my being like a dowry in a chest, coming to my aid, consciously or unconsciously, in countless moments of mothering, householding, living, and loving.

Nina shared many of her grandmother's interests, and carried many of these "motherly" qualities in her being. Now they would not be passed onto another generation of women. Both my mother and my daughter are lost to me in this life. I have to carry the story all alone. Yet, Mom and Nina are now united in the spiritual world, in the core of their beings, in their continuing destiny. Together they will give me the strength and grace to go on nurturing the "eternal feminine" in our now male-dominated family so that it always has a place of honor.

Stories

❧

New Freedom

At the end of the summer of 1999, a phase of my life was coming to an end. My mother had died, Kevin had moved on to his post-high-school Europe experience, and Soren would be starting first grade.

We enrolled Soren in the Minnesota Waldorf School, where Nina and Kevin had gone. It was in Roseville, Minnesota, just two miles from Schroeder Milk Company, where Dennis worked. I had resigned from my teaching position at the Spring Hill School, hoping to move closer to Dennis' work and Soren's school, thus eliminating the commuting craziness from our life.

The Minnesota Waldorf School traditionally holds an all-school picnic on the Tuesday after Labor Day, and then starts school on Wednesday. Dennis, Soren, and I went to this picnic at a park near the school. There we met many new families and renewed acquaintances with other parents and teachers we had known from four years ago when Kevin was in eighth grade. Our association with this school community was strong and deep.

I drove Soren to school on the first day for the opening ceremony. The new first graders gathered with the kindergarten teachers, who led them to the festival hall. Accompanied by the faculty singing and surrounded by beautiful draped silk and flowers, each child walked across a bridge on stage and joined the new class to meet the teacher who would shepherd them through the next eight years of their education. The teacher, Gideon Weick, then told a story to the class of the adventures awaiting them. The eighth graders each presented a new first grader with a red rose. Finally, Mr. Weick led the children to their classroom.

Witnessing this ceremony for the third time with my third child brought up tender emotions for me and Dennis. The beauty of the ritual marking the first day of school, and the fact that our older two had gone through the same ceremony and completed the cycle that was just beginning for Soren, overwhelmed me with feelings of gratitude and sadness at the same time. Tears filled my eyes to overflowing.

The next day, I said goodbye to Soren with his lunch basket in hand as he got in the car to leave with Dennis. When the front door to the house was closed and the breakfast dishes done, I sat down at the computer to begin my new endeavor. The freedom I now had with Soren in first grade opened up the opportunity to write the book that had been gestating in my mind for several months.

It was time to tell my story. I was holding within me the trauma of three years that no mother should have to bear. I had to sift through the details of the places, the people, and the events, and release all that I was holding within to find out what was left of me.

Morning after morning, as I sat at the computer, reliving the details of Nina's life and death, tears streamed down my face. A few hours each morning was enough. I allowed space to reenter my present life, tending to laundry, bills, and errands before I picked up Soren in the afternoon.

Simple Joy

In October, Dennis was planning to go to the Annual General Meeting of the Anthroposophical Society in Denver. Looking over the conference program and the workshops offered, I decided to go with him. Perhaps it would add another dimension to my healing quest. A trip away, alone with Dennis, sounded enticing as well.

I registered for the conference and chose a workshop entitled "Awakening Love, Transforming Selfishness." In preparation for the conference, my workshop leader sent some materials on the theme. Several exercises were suggested for supporting the work toward inner transformation. One involved observing an object from nature in quiet surrender, letting it reveal itself.

Outside my front door many calendula flowers were growing, yet I had never stopped to look carefully at one of them. Calendula plants are not flamboyant in foliage or in flower, so they are easy to overlook. When I plucked a blossom and observed it for a few minutes in the spirit of the exercise, a whole world of unknown secrets opened up to me. The form and color of the flower, its daisy-like golden yellow petals and rich rusty brown center, and the delicate aroma it emitted, filled my senses. A feeling of joy accompanied these sensations. I felt as though Nina was speaking to me through the calendula flower and, at the same time, felt that it was akin to Nina in its simple and unassuming nature.

This experience left me open and expectant to what the weekend in Denver might bring. I especially looked forward to Friday, the day before the conference began, when Dennis had meetings and I was free to do whatever I pleased. With only a vague map, a water bottle and a snack, I headed west to the mountains in our rental car. I followed signs to Red Rock Park. I went up and up on a windy road and finally found a parking area at the Trading Post.

Inquiring at the little store, I found that the proprietors had no trail maps. They assured me that I wouldn't get lost if I followed the trail that departed from and returned to the Trading Post. So merrily I set out for my morning hike, planning to return three hours later, drive back to Denver, and meet Dennis and his cohorts for lunch.

Luckily, there are no other people around. Walking alone, I realized that this is what I wanted—to be in nature and with Nina. I asked no questions of Nina; I simply asked that she accompany me. After an eighth of a mile, the sun beating down from the cloudless blue sky threatened "headache!" I spread my light sweater over my head as a canopy, relaxed my head and facial muscles, and continued walking. I implored Nina to be with me.

The red sandstone desert-like landscape of these mountains was unfamiliar to me, but quiet and peaceful.

My heart, too, began to feel peaceful as I quieted the struggles within. High up above the city, there was a life in the mountains that seemed oblivious to the teeming frenzy of city life below. I felt welcomed as a visitor to be a part of what lived in these altitudes for a few hours. The life there revealed itself to me according to the interest I offered to it. I felt honored and loved.

My path led me through rocky passes and scrubby meadows. One moment, as I rounded a corner, I felt compelled to look back over my shoulder. A little yellow leaf fluttered in the breeze as it was carried sideways to the earth. A message penetrated my being. It was the same simple message I had received from the calendula flower: joy. Explanations or qualifications or directives did not complicate it. Then joy became my gentle companion, expecting nothing of me nor judging me. I knew this was Nina.

I savored this realization within me as the path wound on. I came to a turning point when thoughts of the world began to intrude. "Am I on the right path? Will this take me back to my starting point? Will I get there in time?"

My peace began to leave me when I realized that I had missed the path back to the Trading Post. I had to use my wits to find another way back. I was not so aware of my gentle companion anymore and took several wrong turns before I found the right track. I sighed with relief when the Trading Post came in view.

Safely in the car and on my way back to the conference center, I reflected on my morning experience. Nina dwells in another dimension which knows not time nor place. She is present continuously, yet for me to be aware of her presence, I, too, need to enter a state of mind free from attachment to time or place. I enter that state when in nature, in meditation, or in playing or listening to music; and then there is no separation from Nina.

Miraculously, I arrived at the conference center just as Dennis' meetings let out for the lunch break. Even though the official conference was yet to begin, I basked in the satisfaction that I had already received what I came for.

In my workshop the next day, the leader passed around a box of rocks from which each participant chose one to be used for an exercise. A polished rust colored rock cried out to me to be chosen. I felt the hole in the center that marred its flat surface on one side. I explored the bumps on the other side, seeking explanation. I felt two holes, smaller than and not as gaping as the one on the front. The being of the rock spoke to me and I was in a relationship with a rock, just as I had been with the calendula flower. It spoke to me of myself, not of Nina. I wrote a poem about my kinship with this rock.

I am smooth on the outside
Like this rock.
But, you see, I have this wound
Right in the heart of me.
Perhaps the creases and shadows
Of my countenance
Will tell you also
That I have lived through a destiny of sorrowing.
Turn me over and you may explore my bumpy
     features.

You will find more wounds on my underside, small and
    dark.
Perhaps you will sense the layers of living that molded
    those bumps,
And they will become familiar, and lovable,
For they are me.
And those wounds piercing through to the inside of me—
Perhaps you will see—
At the same time
Are letting out shafts of light
From the glassy depths of eternity.

My wounds were becoming a part of me, and I was
beginning to accept myself as I was.

Three Years

Back in Minneapolis, our Reading for the Dead group was
still meeting once a week. The five of us in the core group
began to marvel that we had been coming together for this
single purpose for close to three years. We were beginning
to feel the effects of that effort of will.

The reading group was the steady current that kept
Dennis and me afloat through all the struggles. The
patient nurturing of a relationship to Nina and the others
across the threshold as spiritual beings had wrought a
slow transformation. Nina became a living being for us,
no longer just the child whom we had lost. That part still
was present, but had receded considerably. If our physical loss was all we based our experience on, we probably
still would have been harboring the pain of that wound.

As it was, we had another reality that helped us to move forward beyond pain.

The reading group felt it was time to share our experience with the community. Because we were transforming the tragedy for the whole community, we needed to give them an "update." Perhaps having a public event was a way to include more people in what we were doing.

Our group invited the community to a celebration of All Soul's Day, celebrated in many cultures on November 2, following "All Hallow's Eve" (October 31) and All Saints Day (November 1) in the Christian calendar. In Mexico it is known as "El Dia de los Muertos" or "Day of the Dead." We gave our celebration the title, "Festival for the Dead: A Community Remembrance."

About thirty people came to participate in this event, including a few students from middle and high school. Softly glowing lights, thoughtful music, and a display of Watershed High School students' altars to their ancestors made in Spanish class welcomed people into the hall on a dark and chilly autumn evening. In the center of the room was a large copper kettle of sand draped with red and gold silk cloths surrounded by pots of rust and yellow colored mums. Each person would be lighting a candle in remembrance to be placed in the sand.

Members of our group led the events of the evening, loosely following the form of our Reading for the Dead group, beginning with a recitation of the verse that we said every week. This was followed by a short excerpt about our connection to those who have died, and a description of the history and purpose of our Reading for the Dead group.

Dennis then led the group, standing in a large circle, in practicing movements for the ceremonial lighting of candles while I played the piano. Then one person lit the first candle and passed the light around the circle until everyone's candle was lit. When the music began, people moved alternately in two groups towards the center, slowly moving their arms up in an arc, then out from the center, arcing back down. After several repetitions, one group at a time knelt in the center to place the candles in the sand, rose, and moved out again. The flames moved up and down with the arms in waves of movement and light. It was a beautiful sight. Many who were there remarked about the spine-tingling experience of coming to the center to place their candles in the sand.

When all the light was gathered into the middle, we encircled it with a long flowing rainbow silk cloth, which each of us held onto. Then, Dennis led us spiraling into the center and out again while we sang, "I am the weaver, I am the woven one, I am the dreamer, I am the dream."

The living and the dead were woven into one great luminous rainbow wreathe, teeming with pulse and breath.

Sitting once again, different people played music or read poetry, while participants absorbed the active portion of the gathering in quietness of soul. As one person extinguished all the candles and we recited the verse again, we held the thoughts of our loved ones within, feeling enriched by this sharing of connectedness.

I felt, through this event, that I was able to give something back to the community for all the love that was given to us throughout our time of loss. By creating a space in our community for recognizing our connection to the dead, our group had also helped to fulfill an important mission.

Eternal Connection

It was a warm, long, drawn-out fall. On the day after Thanksgiving 1999 the calendula flowers outside my front door were still blooming.

On this day, in honor of Nina, I planted bulbs in our front yard—tulips, daffodils, and hyacinth. The third anniversary of Nina's death, this day required simple deeds of remembrance.

As I worked outside, and the sun got higher in the sky, I took my hat off to feel the warmth of the sun. When the job was done, I took off my shoes and socks, carrying them while I walked in the dry grass around to the back door. This is my quiet way of honoring Nina, inspired by a saying by Kahil Gibran. I keep it on my bulletin board and etched in the memory of my heart.

"Forget not that the earth delights to feel your bare feet and the winds long to play with your hair."

This reminds me of the last image Nina left us with in her senior project notebook of a young girl "running wild and alone down a country road." I imagine Nina as a teenager in her wraparound India print skirt, running on the Camphill roads "with her long hair flowing behind her and her strong bare feet thumping firmly on the packed earth." She leaves us with the question, "Why is she running? . . . Is she running to be free or because she is free?"

Another Thanksgiving and another Christmas came and went. All through the fall and winter, I laboriously knitted the sweater Nina didn't get to finish. Though I found the pattern on the borders more challenging than Nina evidently did, I completed it in March at the same time that she began knitting it four years earlier. I was eagerly anticipating wearing it on our trip to Europe. Dennis and I planned to celebrate our 25th wedding anniversary in April with a three-week trip with Soren to Germany, England, and Scotland. Wrapped in the wooly warmth and rich earth colors of Nina's handi-work, I would visit my eldest son on his German farm and Nina's friend, Gwyneth, at Emerson College in Forest Row, England. I would see them beginning to bloom, and meet the people who were helping weave the threads of destiny for them.

In the community of life that was brought into being when we began our marriage, the circles grow ever wider, the colors ever deeper, the threads ever more intricately entwined.

I know now that the stories of Nina and our eternal connection will never end.

Two souls sailing alone in a great sea
were blown together
into the same harbor
to rest.

She gave me the moon
and so have I
given her the
sun.

Now we dance
forever in the moonshine
while sunbeams
gently caress our cheeks.

Poem by Nina Dietzel Artwork by Kirsten Bergh